# Leaves from the Orchard

*Avalonian Connections*

## Alan Royce

First published 2017

Text & Illustrations copyright © Alan Royce, December 2017
Originally edited by Kate Gooch and published as articles in
'Avalon'. http://www.avalonmagazine.co.uk

**All profits from this book have been donated by the author to
support the Library of Avalon, Glastonbury's unique esoteric
library**

Edited and typeset by Penny Billington and Jackie Hosein for
The Library of Avalon, Rear Courtyard. 2-4 High Street.
Glastonbury. Somerset BA6 9DU UK.

Telephone. [UK +44] [0]1458 832 759

librarian@libraryofavalon.org.uk

fb: the library of avalon / friends of the library of avalon

website: www.libraryofavalon.org.uk

Reg. Charity no. 1065014

Cover illustration by Alan Royce
Cover design by Garnet Hosein

The right of Alan Royce to be identified as the author and illustrator
of this work has been asserted.

ISBN: 1974600793

These articles are the author's ongoing researches into many areas of Glastonbury history and spirituality, and the many subjects naturally flow into one another. The editors have made the decision to group them loosely as to theme, but a magazine issue date is supplied to indicate the date of writing.

Dedication

To the original powers and guardians of this special land, long obscured under the Midden of Modern Mythologising centred around the
Magnetic Monikers of Joseph, Arthur and Avalon! May their Green
and Golden Radiance begin to gleam through the Mists once more, for
the blessing of both Realms.

# Contents

# Avalon: Landscape and Myth

# THE CAER OF THE FOUR WINDS

**Alan Royce** *takes us back through the shadows of Time, to a hill wrapped in icy winds without and hiding fiery mysteries within.*

It was an icy, still morning when they climbed the hill. The girl, the woman and the four slaves, breath steaming in the bright sunlight slanting off the glassy pools of the levels, labouring up the hard and slippery track between rime-covered hawthorns. The slaves carried wine and ale in skins and bags of meat and bread, the woman carried her herbs and tinctures and her healers bag. The girl carried their meal, and a small bag with milk and bread for the offering. That was hidden, of course, for the soldiers at the top were Christian men sent by King Caedo and would take umbrage at the older ways.

The slaves grumbled cheerfully and sang a rude song about Taran the Thunderer and the adulterous exploits of the Moon. The woman chided them, the hill was Michael's now and the mention of other owners could cost them an ear, or even a tongue, if they weren't careful.

The soldiers would likely be ill tempered – the icy weather and the hill's winds chilled them to the bone despite their wooden huts and their cook fires. Several of them were fevered, which was why Abbot Cormac had sent the woman on this errand. She had taken the opportunity of bringing the girl along, as it was the best chance she would get to meet the Lord of the Mound and His Lady. She had it all planned out.

The top of the hill was bigger than she recalled. In the middle of a clutter of ramshackle huts stood the remains of the tower of the old temple. The first Christians had used the new laws to get it altered into an oratory of their faith, it being a 'well-constructed fane', but it had never really caught on – too hard to reach and there was no religious reason for the sheep of this new shepherd to make the climb. It was rescued from peaceful decay by Caedo's cavalrymen, sent here to keep an eye on the Saxons down south in Ilchester, or whatever they called the place nowadays. So, several men loitered on this cold summit and kept the beacon fire in good order in case an army of colourful Jutish infantry from Wessex hove into view along the old Roman road.

They and their companions in the cavalry fortlet below were the only people who cared if the Saxons came. The farmers around the old hill fort and sacred woods at Dundon actually traded with them, on the quiet, and Abbot Cormac knew them well. Munster had no quarrel with Saxons.

The men were sitting in the lee of the old tower, playing knuckle-bones and laughing. That made it easier. The sight of the slaves and their Guardians moved them to cheerful shouts – the decurion practised his formal greetings on the woman and the girl, who responded in kind. Formalities drifted into gossip about the Abbot and the mead hall and the boats on the river – was the ice thinning? Could anyone move? No? Ah well, more days of waiting and more stories to share, not so bad really… She told the girl to go and sit in the old tower and get the meal ready while she checked the men's health and gave them the herbs the Abbot had sent – that was all right wasn't it? It was, so she sat by the fire and opened her bag of wares and tools…

The girl did as bidden – the entrance to the tower was in the East, not far from the old fire altar which was stacked with the branches of the beacon fire and kept dry by a cover of dark skins. The tower had no roof and was half full of equipment. The altar in its centre was clear, just a flat stone slab set on the older altar base – just right. She checked that the soldiers were all around the fire with her mistress – they were, she could hear them – and emptied the food bag onto the altar top. This was a good place to prepare dinner; also a good place to hide her real work.

When the meat strips, bread and apples were set out around the table edge, she took out her offerings: two little bowls, some barley bread and a tiny pottery bottle of goat's milk. She kissed the stone, touched her forehead against it and looked deep into the earth with her inner sight. In the glassy depths, the fiery serpents coiled and swam – slow in winter sleep, but present. She sent out the silent call from her heart and poured milk into one bowl and broke bread into the other.

Then she sat behind the altar and made the fire in her heart with her breathing, as her mistress had taught her, and extended the threads of this fire up, down, North, South, East and West and held them there, hot as a sunny day.

She waited, calmly breathing, and the light threads opened into visions of roads. Roads leading far away in every direction through lovely summer lands to great caers, seats of mighty powers upon fertile hills. Sitting at the crossroads she sent out the call. She felt the attention of those in the great caers – their regard held her in a place like four soft winds. She felt as if she were the tree at the heart of the world. The fiery presences below rose up into her own inner fire, the soft glow of the stars above passed down through her, until the link was made, sudden as the lightning, and the owner of the hill was there.

He sat before her inner eye as one of the warriors of the old time. Golden parade armour, sacred patterns and number-knots covering every surface, fierce red hair and moustache, tall helmet, long spear shaft across his knees, eyes compassionate and terrifying in their clarity. And he was smiling the fierce smile of a father proud of his child's achievements.

The girl knew she must speak first. "I have the blood of gold and I have tasted the serpents tongue – bright master, will you show me the way?"

His eyes searched her as if she were the faintest of mist, looking for lights and forms. "I will, little bright one. And you must cherish the knowing and keep it hidden, for a cold rain is to fall for many years and the flame must be kept dry and safe, concealed in the open and hidden on everyone's lips."

The girl felt the riddle, resisted trying to understand, and the Old One reached his hand right into her, saying, "Come." All she knew then was the feeling of utter emptiness and the glimmer of serpents, the whisper of their dreaming tongues. She knew that she was both 'below' and 'within'. She was herself, she was the Land, she was the mighty Goddess of the Land, the threads of whose attention the serpents are, yet she was nothing at all.

She rested, seething as a cauldron does on the hearth fire, allowing herself to cook in her own heat. Slowly, the swirls and eddies began to take form, the threads of the tapestry wove feelings and sensations. Shapes took on meaning. There was a hard floor below her, sky above, birdsong (well, rooks anyway) and a stone table before her, blocking the light from the door. She looked down. At some point she had drawn in the dust, all unknowing, a thing that looked like a letter "T" or a smith's hammer. She wondered what it meant, what had happened when she was in the land. She knew something had been given and she knew it would take time before it would unfold inside her. Such things were like flower buds, they opened in their own good time, at the right season.

She clambered to her feet, looked long at the offerings, and finally decided to pour them on the earth at the doorstep. It felt right, now the altar fires were gone. She dutifully finished the mead – cut the meat, bread and apples into bits and wrapped them again. She hid the bowls and little bottle away and stepped out of the dreaming wreck of the tower. The men were eating and talking with her mistress – herblore and planting times, not all Caedo's men were full-time warriors.

She stood opposite her mistress and showed the food bag. "You've finished?" The eyes emphasised the double meaning.

"Yes mistress, just how you told me." The eyes smiled.

"Good. We'll go then, and eat on the way home".

The decurion touched her shoulder and offered her a cup of the mild ale the slaves had brought. She took it, liking the strong barley taste. "That will help your feet find the way." His eyes smiled too. The girl began to wonder if he was playing double meaning too. It was too much to think about after so long a journey. She thanked him, and they left, the slaves trailing after them.

The view was mind-stopping: from the icy thatched roofs of the abbey and the settlement, leaking smoke from hearths and kitchens, past the bleak ships clustered around the end of the long hill – the old Roman port and the dark causeway, to the endless pools and bare icy trees of

15

the levels. Far off, the white back of the Mendips and the pale cone of the Isle of Frog formed the horizon. The sea was invisible in the bright haze. They walked down slowly and silently, stopping at a clearing below the hill's shoulder to eat. "What did She give you?" said the woman "I can feel the seed in you, what form did it take?" The girl drew the hammer shape in the frost on the earth.

"Good – see that in your inner vision when you want to go within. She will have given you more than that, but it will come to your knowing soon enough – it will speak in you when there is a need."

"He had red hair …"

"Don't! Never speak of what you saw, unless you want it all to die and become mere words." Her eyes were concerned. "That's very important, always remember. Why do you think the bards speak in riddles and poetry? If they got closer to the speech of the world, their Awen would desert them!"

The girl was silent, eyes wide, things were arising in her heart. "Can I talk about the ideas that came up in me?"

"Certainly, but not with everyone. Don't cast your pearls before swine, as these Christians say!"

The girl looked puzzled, everyone knew pigs were sacred, but giving them river pearls as offerings would be foolish and wasteful. She supposed she understood what the saying meant, though. "He says they will call him Gwynn, when the Christians rule everything," she said, dodging a cuff from her mistress and grinning, as they tramped down the icy spine of the tall hill heading for the welcoming rooftops of the little abbey town of Glasempri.

*Avalon Magazine, Issue 25, Autumn/ Winter 2003*

# GLASTONBURY

The heart of the cauldron is no place of comfort,
The maidens who warm it have breath that can sear.
For a year and a day the companion of poisons,
And where is the drop which will make the way clear?

When the flesh of illusion is softened and fallen,
The fat of assumptions is boiled away,
The bright bones of Spirit, no longer encumbered,
Can leap like the salmon into the new day...

*Though the greatest of gifts, the attention of the Powers can be terrifying!*

# MYTHS OF AVALON

*Alan Royce casts a critical eye over some of the Avalon tales, and gives his own interpretation of their meaning and how they came about.*

Living here, we hear much of Glastonbury as the 'Isle of Avalon' – a place which varies from the sacred orchard where the Sun Goddess sits down to rest of an evening, to the place where Arthur was taken to be healed by Morgan and her sisters.

This diversity focuses into the twelfth century Grail Mythos, which has been greatly elaborated since that time – so much so that one is tempted to ask the Grail Question: "What are these things and whom do they serve?"

As for 'Avalon', this is a sort of mediaeval misuse of Old Welsh intended to mean "The Place of the Apples". Apple orchards in the West have an ancient pedigree, generally being a symbolic reference to the 'place' in the afterlife 'ocean' where the Sun Goddess (who is a universal type of the human soul) rests after the short 'daytime' of life. It is a form of the Iranian/Hebrew "Pardes", the Walled Garden of Truth, which becomes "Paradise" is the Christian tradition.

This imagery is unfolded in various ways in Old Welsh sources, and survives in mediaeval collections such as the stories of Rhiannon in the Mabinogion and the Myrddin poem in the Black Book of Camarthen.

Another mediaeval collection – the "History of the Kings of Britain" by Geoffrey of Monmouth – also refers to Avalon as an "island in the sea" to which the wounded King Arthur is taken to heal, so that he can return to this world when needed. Such stories in Geoffrey's time served as different things for different folks – entertainment for the people, propaganda for the elites, and esoteric allegories for the initiated. The Grail stories, which had all these functions, incorporated many of Geoffrey's ideas and took them further.

Queen Eleanor of Aquitaine, a strong supporter of the reforming Troubadour movement, brought these enhanced ideas to Britain, and the links between her Winchester Court and Glastonbury Abbey soon focused many of the stories in this area. The monks, somewhat illogically, decided that the Isle of Glaston must be the Isle of Avalon as they had found (??) the bones of Arthur in their graveyard. Obviously Morgan didn't heal *this* Arthur! It has been suggested that this was why the bones were found – a dead Arthur was emphatically *not* coming back to help the Welsh, who were in serious rebellion at the time.

So Glastonbury became Avalon – at least in the view of Saxon and Norman monastics, who had little access to the deeper meanings of the word.

Who, then, was Morgan, the healer of Arthur? We can have fun with Celtic etymologies here (a venerable sport among esoteric folk). Morgan, in Cornish, means "Sea Shine" – at least on a surface level (pun!). Morgans are Mermaids. This is not very helpful; but, if we recall that the mermaid is half 'Virgin' and half 'Fish', we see that she is a fine symbol of the inner (Virgo) and outer (Pisces) aspects of the Age of Pisces. As Christ was the Master and Initiator of that age, a reference to Christ's deeper teachings is suggested. The form of the 'Sea Virgin' also refers to Classical and Levantine Sea Goddesses like Aphrodite, Atargatis, and even Mary (Mariam – "Mar" being "sea").

These female beings are all related to sacrificial male consorts, upon which Jesus's life was a deliberate reflection. This Eastern line of initiation is linked via the name to its Western equivalents – "Morgan" is like "Morrigan" ("Great Queen" or "Sea Queen"), and "Rigan" is the root of "Rhiannon" ("the Queenly One"), the Sovereignty Goddess of the Irish Colony in Dyfed, South Wales (my own roots).

So Morgan is a masterly esoteric construction. What of Arthur?

There are several facets here. The original Arthur was a post-Roman "Duc Bellorum" ("War Duke") - never a King. However, by the middle ages, he had acquired royal status. It is possible that he is a commentary on what Kings *should* be - a proper spouse of the Sovereign Goddess of his land.

The name may also have been chosen from history by initiates because of its interesting links and puns. "Artor" is related to "Bear". "Arctos" is linked to "North" (as in "Arctic"). These are also puns with "plough" ("Ard") and "high" (as in "Ard-righ" – "High King"). All these little jests point to the importance of the Circumpolar Stars as a symbol. The Great Bear, Little Bear and Dragon are all there, circling around Polaris every night.

Is this King Arthur a King of Souls? In classical thought, souls arose among the stars and fell to earthly bodies via the palaces of the seven great planetary spirits, who provided them with all the soul qualities they would need on earth. This fall, or 'death', had to be reversed for a soul to go home to the stars – to be 'saved'. "Let the Dead bury their dead" was said in this context.

The beauty of the Sea Goddesses concealed the map of the Way Home; their threatening nature was a hint that, to 'ascend', a soul must 'die' to all the given planetary qualities it considered to be itself. Consider Mary of Magdala "out of whom Jesus cast seven devils" – that is, who was liberated from the limitations of the planetary qualities in their earthly forms.

These mysteries were at the heart of the Grail Mythos – a gift brought from the Middle East by the Crusaders and fed by esoteric Judaism and Islam in Spain. They entered Britain via Eleanor's Court, Norman scholarship, French alchemists, Cistercians and Knights Templar. Their popularity as stories spread them all over Europe, and gave Glaston fame as an early source of the Knowledge concealed therein.

Morgan and Arthur are not, therefore, intended to be truly historical beings. Far deeper mysteries are intended. The same is, apparently, true of Joseph of Arimathea, whose story joins that of the others very early on (as a source of lineage). Something deeper and greater than history is intended – but history is a good vehicle for the transmission.

So, Glastonbury may not *actually* be Avalon (nowhere *is*, though many places in Britain are *said* to be). But it certainly conceals a powerful tradition which relates to the Dead and to Spiritual Resurrection (one of the main aims of real alchemy). Ancient Pagan allegories of soul renewal and ascent are recast into potent trans-Christian versions of the same work.

Yes, Glastonbury's legends are truly worthy of careful study. But, for the sake of your soul, do not take them too literally!

*Avalon Magazine, Issue 20, Spring 2002*

# A TEMPLE ON THE TOR?

**Alan Royce** *shares the evidence he has collected and researched from several sources, which indicates that a sacred circular Temple may once have crowned Glastonbury Tor.*

Back along, I went to a talk at the town library at which the Hollinrakes – Glastonbury's resident archaeologists – gave a summary of recent discoveries in the town. Apparently, practically every bit of dry ground out on the Levels was inhabited around 3500 BCE, after which the current layers of raised peat began to form, burying these little islands under a uniform blanket of dead vegetation

Signs of Bronze Age settlement have been found at Chalice Well, along with strong hints that the hilltops were extensively cleared and farmed even then, as they were in the Middle Ages. Roman settlement was common around the Safeway area and around Wearyall Hill, with a large 'high status' building somewhere in the Abbey grounds.

The Abbey itself abounds in untouched archaeology. The odd fragments of road, pond, ditch etc. uncovered in small-trench examinations suggest a sizeable and well-planned Saxon town here long before the Norman 'new town' was set up around the 1200's and the Abbey moved to its present site.

All this was intriguing – especially the occupations on the Levels (my favourite period is the Neolithic). But the *piëce de rësistance* was the re-interpretation of the data from the 1963 dig on the Tor-top in the light of a recent geological survey. This stated that the Tor-top is in fact very stable, so a curved foundation trench can no longer be seen as a distorted remnant of a straight footing for the first church, but must be the base of a circular building. This is thought to be the remnant of a Romano-Celtic temple – not unreasonable given the prominent site and the sizeable Roman occupation.

The finding of many ammonites and a greenstone Neolithic axehead tie the temple into a group of cult sites centered on the Paris area and spreading out along trade routes. The curious absence of votive objects etc. usually linked to such sites may be explained by a rather well-hidden dig carried out in 1879 by local pioneering excavator Bulleid, the finds from which are apparently stored in Taunton and have not been seen for generations!

I must say that I was not desperately convinced by all this, but the idea is an intriguing one. I copied out the 1963 general plan of the Tor-top and coloured in the objects and trenches, etc. relevant to the temple. I then found its ritual centre as best I could, and measured angles out from there. The results of this tomfoolery made me take much more notice of the idea.

As you can see, the stone axe, the bronze head and the 'cross base' show remarkable signs of being deposited in an orderly manner relevant to the temple centrepoint (subject to the imprecisions of my drawings, of course). It would be very interesting to do a similar analysis on the other site-plans for this cult-grouping to see if any consistent system is being followed.

As for the separate items in the layout, once you go beyond the simple idea that there is an orderly pattern (and that the Eastern porch suggests both a door and an interest in Sun and Moon rises) things get very speculative. However, being neither archaeologist nor academic professional, I'm allowed to speculate freely (and to be spectacularly wrong!). That being said, let's look at the site from another viewpoint.

The drawing on the next page summarises these findings in a simple manner.

One of the finest sources for the kind of culture and mindset predominant in Celtic days is the current pagan revival material from Lithuania. This country speaks one of the oldest Indo-European languages (with roots predating both Celtic and Germanic language groups) and retained a functional pagan culture up until the 18th century. It enshrines a huge 'archive' of old European pagan world-views and practices, and, more to the point, its calendar is quite similar in form and spirit to later 'Celtic' calendar forms. So, freely borrowing from Lithuanian and Roman models, let's look at the finds.

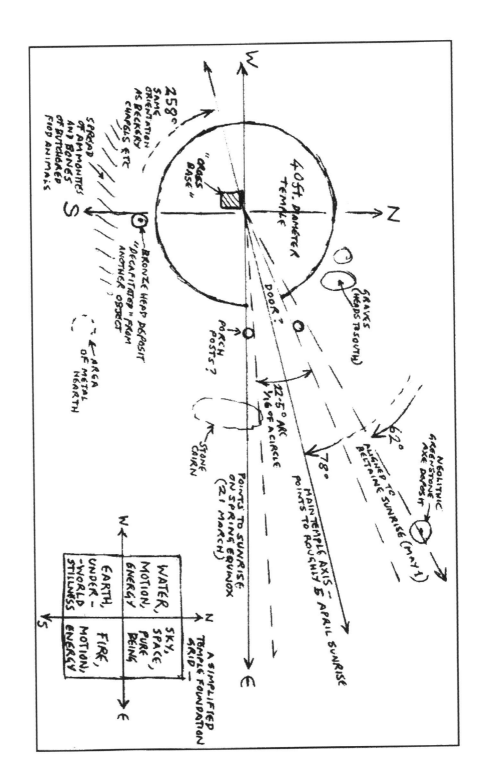

W

258°
SAME
ORIENTATION
AS DECKERY
CHASSES ETC

SPREAD
OF AMMONITES
AND BONES
OF BUTCHERED
FOOD ANIMALS

S

BRONZE HEAD DEPOSIT
"DECAPITATED" FROM
ANOTHER OBJECT

AREA
OF METAL
HEARTH

405t. DIAMETER
TEMPLE

N

"GLASS
BASE"

DOOR ?

PORCH
POSTS ?

STONE
CAIRN

STAKES
(HEADS TO SOUTH)

22·5° ARC
1/16 OF A CIRCLE

POINTS TO SUNRISE
ON SPRING EQUINOX
(21 MARCH)

62°

78°

ALIGNED TO
RECTAINE SUNRISE (MAY 1)

NEOLITHIC
GREENSTONE
AXE DEPOSIT

MAIN TEMPLE AXIS —
POINTS TO ROUGHLY IS APRIL SUNRISE

E

A SIMPLIFIED
TEMPLE FOUNDATION
GRID —

| | N | |
|---|---|---|
| W | WATER, MOTION, ENERGY | SKY, SPACE, PURE BEING |
| | EARTH, UNDER- WORLD STILLNESS | FIRE, MOTION, ENERGY |
| | S | E |

**The Temple Building.** Circular, about forty feet in diameter, probably with a porch in front of a door facing about 10 degrees North of East. The 'cross base' and several small pits, mostly West of it, seem to lock into the pattern of incoming sunrays from the door in interesting ways. Were they all parts of the original building? The 'cross base' could have supported a small altar, an image or a 'sacred flame' such as was reported at Bath. It could even have borne a cross later when the site was adapted for Christian use (by Papal decree?).

Note the wheelcross head broken off and buried nearby – a result of the change from 'Western Orthodox' to 'Roman Catholic' Christianity when the Saxons took over in 650 or so? As for its pre-Christian meaning, it sits completely within the South West quadrant of the temple space – the area dedicated to Earth, Ancestors and Stillness. Sun shining on such an altar would imply the idea of light entering the darkness of death and enlivening it in some way. The ray of light which would have fully illumined this altar would have come in through the door at sunrise around 5th April – the middle of the range of possible dates for the Lunar feast at which the dead were given into the hands of the deity of illumination (and thunder and lightning!) to be escorted to the blessed realms of the Ancestors. This feast was determined in the same way as the original Easter (indeed, its later Saxon form was called Ostara) by the first full moon after the Spring Equinox.

My feeling is that the whole orientation of the space and the angles subtended by the porch post-holes combine to emphasise this 'Guide and Guardian of the Blessed Dead' function of the Young Thunder and Lightning God. One is reminded of the 'Leucetius' honoured at Bath with his partner 'Nemetona' – 'Lightning', husband of 'Sacred Grove'.

Lightning is still a symbol of the power of spirit-consciousness in traditions throughout Britain. Perhaps the temple served to ritually raise the year's dead from their dormant or underworld state (their 'Winter') to the divinely illumined state symbolised by 'Summer'. The Egyptians did the same for *their* dead, raising them to celestial heights in the hope of a grateful return gift of prosperity and spiritual help.

As for the holes – *if* they were part of the temple – maybe they represent sockets for sunsighting poles, or little deposits of vegetation honouring the meanings of specific points of time. Such things were done. The ancestors in the earth empowered all surface life; so, messages we-re sent to them (and the surface life attuned to them) by putting things into the ground. This was a way of showing those below what powers to send up through the soil to their descendants. This concept is import-ant in looking at the next items – the deposits outside the building.

**The Greenstone Axehead.** This Neolithic axe, known in folklore as a 'Thunderstone', is buried on the line of the May Day (Beltaine) sunri-se as seen from the temple centre. It shows the date at which the Thun-der God of Spring hands over to the powers of Summer. Such axes were used, along with later hammers (e.g. those of Celtic Sucellos or Germanic Thorr) to 'hallow' spaces, objects and people, and to promote health, purity and fertility. The waters in Lithuania were impure until 'seined' by thunder and lightning, after which they became a purifying force. The placing of Thunderstones in water is a ritual remnant of this idea and is a widespread concept in Europe – see even the witch's rite of placing the knife (originally a spearhead) into the cup to enliven its contents with spirit. Another curious remnant of this idea can be seen in the Rural Life Museum at Glastonbury – the 'Luckstone' is a fine little image of the Thunder Axe and its indwelling spirit of Light and Awareness. Such things have been found in old Ireland.

**The Bronze Head.** This is fascinating. It is a small bronze face, mounted on an iron backing, broken off some object and buried in the soil due South of the central point of the temple. It seems to me to combine three ideas. First, it is a reminder of Janus as the Doorkeeper of the old and new Solar years at Midwinter (the South is where the Sun goes in Winter, the North where it heads in Summer – the 'Summer Lands' and the 'Summer Stars').

Second, it is a sacred, decapitated head in the full Celtic tradition, containing the essence of the function of the object of which it was a part – in this case perhaps a tub, bucket or cauldron holding sacred fluid of some kind (don't ask!).

Third, it is a protective head, warding off potential evils from both the symbolic and the actual South. Similar heads – in this case real skulls – were buried in boundary ditches at Windmill Hill, Avebury, as spirit guardians.

**The Ammonites and Bones.** These seem to have been mainly found in the Southern range of the hilltop outside the temple wall. The ammonites have several connotations, all of which could have relevance in context. Firstly, they are coiled 'serpents'. Serpents are symbols of ancestral presence; coiled serpents are these energies at rest or in potential. The idea of the Kundalini Serpent coiled at the base of the spine is strongly related. They could be the newly dead resting in the Southern earth.

Secondly, they are the coiled ram's horns of the God of the East, the awakener of nature and spirit. The very name 'ammonite' derives from the horns of 'Zeus Ammon', the enlivening spirit of the sky in Greek/Levantine lore.

As an aside, the small metal hearth found nearby is fully in context. One of the powers of the East is smithcraft, and the Lithuanians have stories about the Disc of the Sun being reforged at Midwinter (Midwinter Sunrise?). Indeed, what other trade would a hammer-god practice?

There is also a Goddess connection. The horned animals are symbols of *consorts* of the source of spiritual powers at the heart of the earth – the Goddess's guardians and servants at various stages and functions of the year. There are remnants of this in the cycle of Summer and

Winter Gods fighting over the 'Inner Sun', the Goddess of the Land's life. The local tale of Gwynn, Gwythyr and Creiddyladd is directly relevant and set in the same time-frame as the temple (last part of Spring).

The bones will be the remnants of feasts – whether the site was dedicated by holding one, massive feast for the ascending dead or whether there were many smaller ones, we do not know. This feast for the dead is the pagan precursor of Easter, and would have been easily converted to its Christian counterpart when that faith came to predominate. Perhaps the temple set some local precedent – the alignment of the burials and chapels on Beckery in Saxon times are orientated to the same date /direction as the temple.

Though the temple generally suggests a seasonal rite of renewal relating to the land and the ancestors, the same site could have been used for the inner equivalents of this work. It could have been an initiation site for people with the potential for priestly mediation or for rites connected to the religious functions of Kings. The small size of the Tor-top suggests it was used by limited numbers of people, and was thus quite specialised. One is tempted to ask where the big, public sacrifice sites on the island were…

So, to summarise, I'm inclined to believe in this temple, and I'm intrigued that it fits so neatly into the local traditions. The first church on the Tor is dedicated to Michael – a being of spiritual light and a guide for the souls of the dead – and (probably) to Brigit – a nurturing and culture-bearing presence related to cows, milk, ale and the seasonal behavior of serpents! The theme is continued by the deliberate importation of the Gwynn ap Nudd story from the Life of St. Collen.

One suspects that the transition from Leucetius, the hammer-god and psychopomp, to the angelic companions of Yeshu the Anointed One, was reasonably gradual and possibly quite amicable.

*Avalon Magazine, Issue 21, Summer 2002*

# BORDERLANDS

**Alan Royce** *considers the Powers of the Land – and
the significance of water in the sacred landscape.*

I've heard it said that Glastonbury is more like some frontier town than
the heart of British Christianity. Certainly there are days when it has
that kind of feel. We had similar places back home in Essex; Jaywick
Sands on a stormy autumn day could be quite surreal... Of course, there
are differences. Somerset does a fine job of raised peat-bog and will-
ow-lined rhynes, while we specialised in endless creeks and salt marsh
and curlews and bracing winds straight off Siberia. Sometimes I get
quite homesick!

In fact, the two counties have a lot of half-hidden things in common.
Both are fluctuating borderlands between land and sea, both have the
Saxon tongue laid over an older, Brythonic culture, both have the Old
Manner of Faith just a few inches below the surface. I'm not speaking
of the city folk, the Bristol men, the Londoners. How many of them
look below the surface of their 'stones piled upon stones' (as Wulfstan
said of the new Norman churches of his day)? I'm speaking of the folk
who had to get up in the night to hare around lighting tar barrels in the

orchards to stop frost killing the crop, or kids like me who spent autumn days out in the fields stacking straw bales until our forearms ran with blood. It's hard to know the land until you have made this kind of offering.

And this brings me to my actual subject.

On moving here, I did the honourable thing and asked the Powers of the Land if I had their permission to work here, a long process which led me to Dundon Beacon, Wookey Hole Caves, and finally the Sulis Minerva temple in Bath. There I was given my permission and told to concentrate on 'the wells to the west of Glaston'. Of this more later, as you will see, but an offering was proper at Sul's great spring. A silvery five pence was fine, it having been made the vehicle of the proper energy and intent. We were most amused, on following one of the tours through the throngs of visitors, to hear a guide telling folk that this had once been an immensely popular location for people making religious vows or offerings, but that it happened no more. The poor lambs must be either singularly unobservant or constrained to a company script!

But, back to the wells. I did go and visit the ones I could reach, and found them both inspiring and malodorous, for several are sulphur wells.

The ancient Greeks used sulphur and sea-water to purify sacred places, a bit like the New Age use of sage smudging, so these self-purified locations must have had an inherent sanctity. Connect this with the likelihood that a trade/pilgrim road linked all these wells, and the area starts to look interesting. I noted that the route was reflected in the Roman road network and in later Christian pilgrimage routes, but I more-or-less stopped there – a sacred roadway across a huge, and probably sacred, bog. Polden begins as Pouholt Estate. Pouholt may derive from *Pwll-Hollt*, Welsh for 'Split Pool', which is at least appropriate, no?

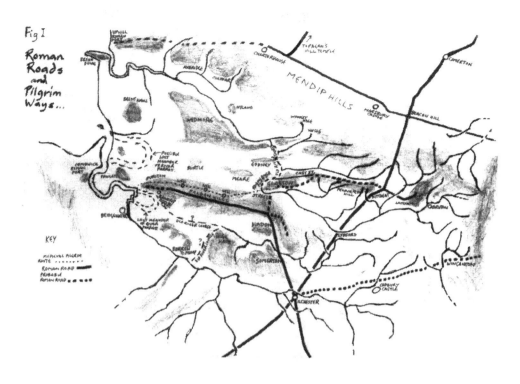

Fig I

Roman Roads and Pilgrim Ways...

KEY

MEDIEVAL PILGRIM ROUTE ········
ROMAN ROAD ▬▬▬▬
PROBABLE ROMAN ROAD ▪▪▪▪

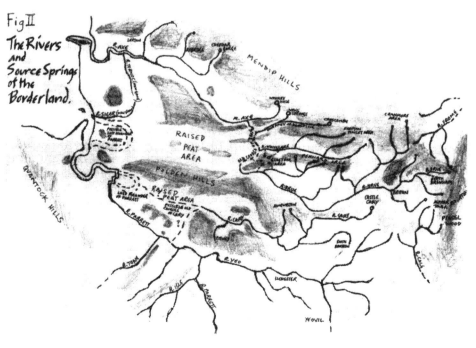

Fig II

The Rivers and Source Springs of the Borderland.

My attention was drawn back to the area more recently when work with the land-spirits was re-emphasised, and my long-term interest in 'naming the Old Gods of Glaston' re-awoke. The two projects are not one, as the Land-wights soon pointed out, but the one informs the other in interesting ways. For instance, the vital importance of natural features in pre-Roman cults was emphasised, especially the significance of river watersheds, confluences, estuaries and source springs.

This in itself was work enough – try to find a map which shows all a river's tributaries, or the palaeo-channels now buried under silt or bog.

However, it has given a wondrous insight into *why* the Romans did *what* they did *where* they did.

At this point I came across the work of Stephen J. Yeates, who has collected and made sense of mountains of data about the Dobunni tribe and their Hwicca descendants. He, too, emphasises watersheds and River Goddesses. It is intriguing when land-spirits and scientists speak the same language. He also writes of a Goddess perceived as the Mother of all the Dobunni. She appears on many stone reliefs, accompanied either by her consort, the 'Celtic Mercury', or by those three strange cloaked beings, the 'Cucullati'. This Mother of the Dobunni (the 'people of the vessel'?) holds a ladle over a big cylindrical vessel. The vessel's nature is unclear – indeed, it can vary – but water bucket, milk-churn, cooking cauldron or wine/mead container seem the main options.

'The Ladle' is an old name for the stars at Ursa Major, which may suggest a stellar component to Her myth, and will no doubt stir memories in those who have read Robert Cochrane's, or Doreen Valiente's, work.

We could take this further if we opt for the milk-churn idea and extend this into the Milky Way. We could even wonder whether our local Matrona is represented by the image on Glaston Tor of 'Bridget milking her cow' amid streams of water, mist or stars?

BRIGID AND HER COW To the right, above the Tor Trunk Door facing S.W.

Comparisons with the figures on the Gundestrup Cauldron arise ... the woman at the lowest point of the Milky Way and the man about to be immersed in a vessel at the highest point. Here in the Dobunni lands a Mother owns a vessel, and some significant burials (so says Yeates in Tribe of the Witches, p.137, Dreaming for the Witches, p.159) are found with 'vessels over their heads'. Remarkable common imagery and more fuel for the 'Milky Way – White Cow' hypothesis.

Are we looking at a seasonal filling and emptying of great landscape 'vessels' (Yeates suggests the circular valley north of Gloucester, I would add the Somerset Levels around Glaston) in whose contents the 'Stars in the Underworld' are made visible by reflection? Stars have long been symbols of that seed-point of potential illumination, the human soul.

Now, here is a true story. In my early years here I went up one night to the top of the Tor. At midnight, the proper time, I made an offering of milk and grain to the Power of the place, and asked for a sign. Up there in the silent air my vision was drawn to the stars overhead, Ursa Major and Cassiopoeia. I haven't understood that answer until now.

33

The Old Gods don't hide, they are just beyond the sticky veils of our habitual self-obsession. The tiniest act of sacrifice, of giving away a bit of that self-obsession, allows chinks of light to come through the musty curtains.

But back to our subject. Where *were* the borderlands of the Dobunni? To my amusement, right where we live – and there was I thinking Glaston's river port served as part of the Durotrigan river-trade system ('Durotriges' can be read as 'Water Dwellers' or as 'Water Kings' – I think the latter is more their style).

The actual border seems to have been the limits of the Axe-Brue watershed, given that the River Axe (Axe = *Isca* = Fish) was effectively a small tributary of the Brue (Berw or *Bryw* = turbulent, boiling, or *Berw Dwr* = watercress, or *Briva* = a brushwood causeway or wooden bridge like that between Lantokay and Northover in late Roman times). Mind you, the last name could suggest that Brue might once have meant only 'the river upstream of the causeway' – hence Bruton and Brewham?

Of course, the Brythonic love of economical speech and puns might have intended all three meanings, as most can be made to fit.

The area I had already got to know was clear enough, the Romans had put a road more-or-less along the boundary line, atop the Polden Ridge. To the north was gently sloping farmland. to the south a steep, wooded scarp, a natural version of the venerable ditch-and-bank defence, and thus a fine symbolic wall around a 'country as hill fort'. This scarp wriggles southwards around Dundon Camp, towards Somerton; then the slopes become gentle, and the watershed turns east through Kingsweston and Keinton Mandeville towards Castle Cary. Castle Cary is interesting.  The source springs of the River Cary (*Cari* = dear, beloved, *Carv* or *Carw* = deer, as in fallow deer, *Cario* = to bear or carry, but this may be a modern loan-word) arise to the south of the little town. Katherine Maltwood speaks of these wells as, I seem to recall, Mary wells, and reports a 'British camp' near to them. Certainly one would expect a border shrine and a river-source shrine here. Another border shrine ought to be at Lydford somewhere, as the Fosse Way crosses both Brue and Cary here. The Fosse is the troop road of a Roman *Limen*, a sort of symbolic defensive border which was open to trade but easily closable in time of conflict. It deliberately crosses all the more natural east-west routes in the area for quick access to all watersheds.

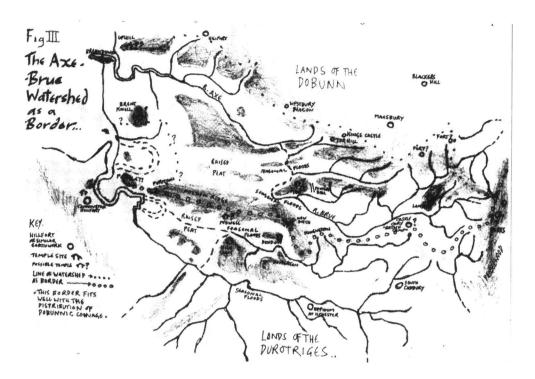

The trade function of the Fosse was deeply significant. Rome conquered in two main ways. Firstly it would champion the introduction of monetary economies in the tribes it encountered. Then it would create a dependency on this type of trade, and, when the climate was right, it would take advantage of a convenient internal dispute to 'help' the losing party with a few of its legions – the second method of conquest. When the tribe had thus been assimilated, its internal structure was altered by the setting-up of Roman-style forts, towns, roads etc., to make it more useful to the Empire.

Interestingly, this process did not die out with the Roman Empire – ask any indigenous culture today for their story.

Beyond Castle Cary the watershed dips south, to include a Brue tributary, and grazes the edge of the Stourhead springs complex to approach the source of the Brue near South Brewham, where finds of votive objects suggest the presence of a shrine. This general area is also a source of the River Frome, and the location of a couple of middling hill-forts, not to mention Bruton and the temple site at Lamyatt to its north-west.

Lamyatt seems to mean 'border gate' or perhaps 'clay gate' in Anglo-Saxon.

A probable Roman road runs from here to the Fosse at Ditcheat (ditch-gate?) and thence across or around Pennard Hill (*Pen-Ard* = high head in Celtic, *Pen-Geard* = cattle-pen yard in Saxon) via East Street to Norwood Park and Dod Lane, through the Abbey to the riverside along Benedict Street (which was once called Mede Lode, or middle jetty).

Glaston, though not on the actual border, may have been part of a significant landscape full of major springs. Both the Glaston peninsular and Pennard have springs worth venerating, and shrines of some sort are to be expected. Glaston as a name, however, may come from the word 'glast' being applied to the great seasonal lake to its north, which the lake villages exploited. So, at least, suggests Yeates.

The Romans, however, seem to have messed up the original, elegant, natural boundary when they gave the southern parts of the Dobunnic lands to their Belgic allies from the east. This seems to have been partly to reward their co-operation, partly to exploit safely the lead in the Mendips, and partly to consolidate a military corridor to the River Severn, where they maintained a serious naval presence.

The Nodens temple at Lydney Park, over the water in the Forest of Dean, seems to have been financed by these navy types, although Nodens himself is portrayed as a form of Mars and may be a God mediating local iron production and its use in the various defence establishments of the area ... the Old God who armed the Dobunnic warriors, now thanked by the invading Romans for the iron in their own weapons.

The more things change, the more they remain the same.

So, we continue to wipe the dust from these ancient things. For some reason pertaining to our own day the land-spirits seem to think this material, and work connected with it, is important. The work is by no means complete, so anything could happen. Do join in if you feel called to do so.

*Avalon Magazine, Issue 44, Spring 2010*

Interlude

# THE BIRDS OF RHIANNON

**Alan Royce** *traces the story of the Celtic*
*Rhiannon back into the distant past.*

In that mysterious collection of late mediaeval tales called the Mabinogion, King Brân the Blessed leads an expedition of Ireland to avenge
the dishonour done to his sister Branwen.

It all goes badly wrong, and Brân is wounded in the foot by a poisoned
dart. Dying, he commands his men to behead him and take his head to
the White Mount in London, to be buried as a magical guardian against
invasion. On the way, in a fascinating journey through Otherworld
Wales, his severed head entertains the company just as it did when he
was alive – to the accompaniment of the singing of the Birds of
Rhiannon, far out over the sea ... birds whose music, it was said, could
'lull the living to sleep and wake the dead'.

Now, it has been said that the tale of Brân's talking head is but a rewri-
ting of the tale of the death of Orpheus, and that the singing of the birds
is merely that heard from the various bird islands off the South Wales
coast – 'Islands in the Otherworld Sea' and 'Soulbirds' implied in a real-
life phenomenon.  But can we say more?

Who, for instance, is Rhiannon? She features in two of the four branches of the Mabinogion, numbers one and three, but in these sections her
symbolism is strongly Horse, not Bird.

In the first branch she is an Otherworld King's daughter, who chooses
a mortal husband rather than be wed to the man selected for her. This
causes a feud which manifests in the stealing of her first child. In a
bizarre series of scenes, her six handmaids accuse her of eating the
boy, smearing the blood of slain puppies on her to 'prove' their point,
and she is punished by being made to behave like a horse, carrying
visitors into the palace on her back. Meanwhile, her baby son is rescued by a nearby chieftain and symbolically twinned with his foal,
born on the same night. The branch ends with mother, son and foal
being reunited, and all being well.

The names are interesting.

'Rhiannon' seems to be a contraction of a Gaulish/Brythonic word Rig-antona/Rigatona', which translates as something like, 'Queenly Godd-ess' (the 'ona' suffix usually indicating a Goddess epithet).

'Pwyll', her mortal husband, translates as 'sense', as in common sense or prudence. A bit of Cymric humour, this, as he singularly lacks both at times.

'Pryderi', her son, simply means 'worry' or 'anxiety' – quite appropriate in the circumstances.

Now, if we look at her story as a sequence of images and notions, we find that she maps rather well onto the genuine Gaulish Goddess of the Roman period, called Epona ('Ep' meaning horse, and 'ona' meaning Goddess, as already stated).

> Both are called 'Queen'.
> Both are portrayed as riding a great horse sidesaddle.
> Both are shown with two foals.
> Both are linked to the fertility of the land.

There are differences, of course. Rhiannon is part of a twelfth-century esoteric story-cycle akin to grail astrology, while Epona is a proper Romano-Celtic Goddess with cult, shrines and temples; but even the differences are instructive.

Rhiannon, for example, wears a 'golden garment' as she rides past Pw-yll and his men. She is also linked to sacrificed puppies. These do not seem to be Epona symbols, as far as I have yet discovered.

Epona, on the other hand, has been portrayed with four foals rather than two on occasion. Unless the 'Four Branches' are vestiges of this, it doesn't turn up in Rhiannon tales.

EPONA WITH TWIN FOALS

THE DIOSCURI AS TWIN HORSEMEN    NOTE THEIR "EGGSHELL" CAPS

THE DIOSCURI WITH THEIR SISTER
HELEN — ALSO BORN OF AN EGG!

Rhiannon is also linked to the sea, both in folklore and in the Four Branches. Her birds sing far out over the Severn estuary; her second husband is Manawyddan ('he of the Isle of Man') – strong hints of Neptune, or the older Poseidon here.

Is there something older and deeper beyond all this?

Well, the fact that the Four Branches are marginal grail lore, and the grail is something 'found in the Zodiac by Jewish and Arab astrologers' according to Wolfram von Eschenbach, is a big clue.

Both the late Roman cults and the Arab astrologers were obviously affected by ancient Greek lore, so we could look there to see what might be found.

Greek horse-lore is complex and old. Consider beings like the Centaurs and Silenoi and Satyrs. Consider Poseidon, who begins as general 'plants and waters' God and becomes Lord of the Sea, Earthquakes, and Horses. Consider Medusa and Demeter, both of whom were said to have mated with him in horse form.

Can we see a late reflection of this in Rhiannon and Manawyddan? Where do Horse, Woman and Sea combine in the Zodiac?

The best fit is the arrangement of Andromeda, Pegasus and Pisces, stars which would rise out of the East after sunset around Harvest-End and fill the Southern sky by midnight. A fine prototype for Pwyll's vision of a slow-riding maiden and a likely source of Epona's 'side-saddle rider' icons.

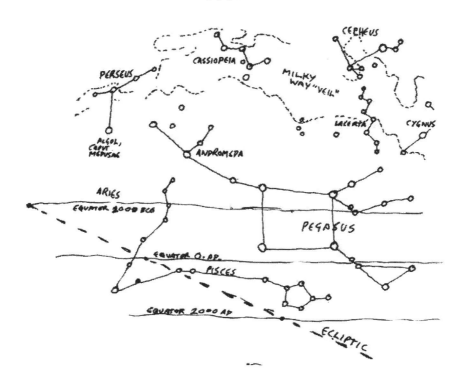

THE AREA OF STARS WHICH THE EPONA AND RHIANNON IMAGES ARE COMPOSED FROM —

But what of the twin foals?

There are several ways open here. The simplest answer is the Dioscuri, Castor and Pollux, the twins fathered on Leda by Zeus in Swan form. These boys were born of an egg, were famous horsemen and helpers of travellers (especially seafarers), and were early-on portrayed as serpents on vertical poles (a possible origin for the Gemini glyph). However, there may be earlier and more celestial answers to the riddle.

The key is the story of Medusa, the 'Guardian'.

Medusa is the mortal Gorgon, one of three sisters. The others were Sthenno ('Strong One') and Euryale ('Wide Stepping'). Their Gorgon title has numerous odd implications, 'Maiden' and 'Pivot Point' being but two of them. Two of these 'Pivot Maidens' are immortal, unchanging, eternal. One is mortal, changeable, impermanent. This one is killed by Perseus with his 'Harpe', a hooked sword, a kind of scythe or pruning hook. Her head sits over the Pleiades, in the space above the Taurus/Aries cusp. This was the Spring Equinox point around 2100 BCE. Is Medusa's story that old? Can we posit, as an experiment, that Medusa guarded the crossover point between the celestial equator (the heavenly analogue of our horizon and the celestial version of the river Okeanos which flowed around it) and the ecliptic circle – the Zodiac?

This leaves her other sisters, from whom her head has been separated, the guardianship of the crossover between the ecliptic and the Milky Way. Probably one looked to the visible stars of the Milky Way, peaking at the Pisces/Aquarius cusp, while the other looked to the invisible stars of same, bottoming around the Leo/Virgo cusp in the Underworld.

In later Medusa lore, the blood from her neck is split into left and right halves. The former kills, the latter revives. Asklepios the Healer keeps it in his constellation Ophiuchus, above Scorpio. This blood, where it touched the ground, became serpents; Asklepios holds serpents.

Also born from the neck of Medusa are Pegasus and Chrysaor ('Golden Sword'), portrayed as winged horse and giant warrior or winged boar. These are Medusa's twin sons by Poseidon, liberated by an unconventional Caesarian section. Quite possibly, all these variants speak of the same thing: two streams of power flowing out of a source at the (then) Spring equinox, and meeting at their opposite point on the Zodiac in the hands of Ophiuchus.

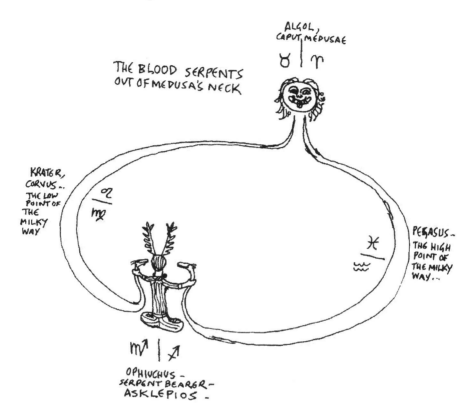

Our Serpent/Horse/Bird twins, the Dioscuri, may be another version of this concept, given that one is mortal, the other immortal. The tale in which Zeus gave them the right to alternate between Hades and the Heavens, when one was killed in battle, was used as a core myth in 'immortalisation' initiations into the Mysteries.

45

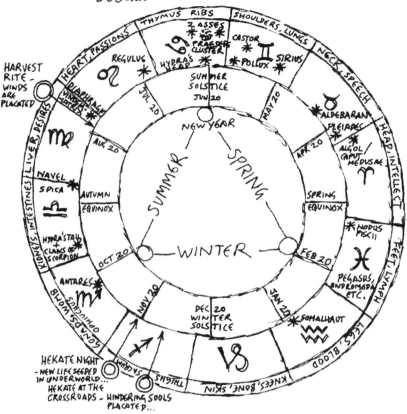

THE 3 HEKATE FESTIVALS MAPPED ONTO THE ANCIENT GREEK YEAR AND THE BODY.. STARS AS AT 500 B.C.E

This can all be mapped onto the body in the standard way using the Zodiac, but the body can also sit upright in the centre, becoming the central oak around which the Serpent/Horse/Bird phases of the soul endlessly process. This central oak which connects and nourishes the worlds can be called Hekate, which would neatly account for Rhiannon's golden garment (Hekate's Saffron Robe), and the sacrificial puppies at Rhiannon's son's birth (the yearly 'Hekate at the Crossroads' rites, when the sun stood in Sagittarius and Gemini stood in the South at midnight, and black puppies were offered in the rite to appease any of Hekate's swarm of souls who might want to impede the conception of next year's fertility and health).

We might even step further back, to 4300 BCE when the equator, ecliptic and Milky Way all met at one point, when the three Crossroad-Guardians, the Gorgons, were only one being – a facet of a single mother who controlled the flow of souls in and out of the Underworld, whence all arises.

Perhaps she was called Hekate then, for the name is old and its etymology puzzling.

But does this bring us nearer to the distant Birds of Rhiannon and their world-bridging songs? As birds are in general heavenly souls and our story is a late one, I would go for our Serpent/Horse/Bird twins, the Dioscuri, who were so intimate with the roads between Hades and Heaven and were the special Gods of those who crossed Okeanos, both in his material form, the sea, and as gateway to the immortal stars.

*Avalon Magazine, Issue 40, Autumn/Winter 2008*

# Avalonians And Their Searches

# THE PERFUME OF THE ROSE

*Since I moved to Glastonbury in 1995, I have been in a position to learn somewhat of the town's history. Not always willingly, I have been led to unearth a number of things about Glastonbury's past which paint a rather curious and fascinating picture.*

I want first to talk about overlays. Glastonbury is a fine example of multiple overlays placed on an already potent and enlivening landscape. Every human culture and period places an overlay upon the land, but this is usually more or less unconsciously created by the demands of everyday life and consciousness. More rarely, aware individuals or groups will feed ideas and forms into their culture's consciousness in order to harness the power of a place to a specific end. This end can be benevolent or tyrannical, depending on the nature of the perpetrators. It can also be long or short lived, stable or unstable, depending on the capabilities of its makers.

In Glastonbury, at least three such overlays can be discerned. The most powerful, yet the most elusive, is that attunement of the land done in Neolithic times. I won't even speak of this, though it is my own favourite.

The next noticeable layer relates to the long work of the Christian monks, both Celtic and Roman Catholic; they are virtually omni-present, after all, the land was theirs for about 1400 years, maybe longer. The "stresses" imposed on the power of the land by their prayers, their ideas, their architecture and the mass mind of an endless stream of pilgrims colours many locations. The stories they fed into people's minds are easily found. Gildas and Patrick, David and Beuno/Benignus, Collen and Bridget are all saints whose lives are claimed as part of Glastonbury's history. Glastonbury Abbey grew wealthy and influential due to their devotees. Later, the tales included Joseph of Arimathea as a visitor, even a founder, and the bones of an Iron Age ruler said to be King Arthur were found. The landscape bears relics of this work. On the Tor is a church dedicated to St Michael, supposedly put there to keep down the Old Serpent – an appropriate "capping" for a mighty old Dragon Hill! At Beckery, a chapel once dedicated to the Magdalene was rededicated to Bride, St Bridget, who apparently came to visit Patrick, when he was Abbot of the Celtic anchorites here, and left her bell and some weaving gear to be treasured later as relics. The chapel lived on until the Dissolution as a place of pilgrimage.

The Holy Thorn marked the place where Joseph the Tinman planted his staff on arrival at the Roman river-port at Wearyall Hill; more likely it was bought here by Crusaders or later folk – it only lives 100 years or so in this country and has to be propagated, being unable to self-seed in our climate.

The Abbey itself has crept eastwards over the centuries. The Old Church, more or less the present Mary Chapel, was at first the symbolic "East" of the colony, its spiritual origin, the "sunrise" point of truth. Over the centuries, grand churches were built further to its east, until the Mother of God had her house in the West. Much of the imagery of the Blessed Mother of God arises from this Western "sunset" sea.

Along with this change came mystical knowledge from the Middle East, from the newly formulated Jewish Qabalah and the ancient Chaldaean gnosis, quarried and transmuted by Islam and brought back by crusaders. In France, crusader courts became centres of learning; troubadours arose as did Courts of Love. Islamic culture flowed into Christendom, mostly in a veiled form, but pervading everything. Christianity was transformed, sometimes hideously, when it reacted violently against the flow of change, sometimes rising to sublime heights. The fusion of many levels of ancient story into the Grail Myths was one of the ways in which the new knowing was transmitted.

Glastonbury shows signs of having been bound up in these changes. The Abbey had strong links to the French courts and had long been an almost independent state within England. Jack Gale's fascinating "*The Circle and the Square*" deals with just this theme – recommended reading!

At the dissolution, this complex overlay was traumatically disrupted, apparently leaving a kind of "wound" which is only yet beginning to heal properly.

There is another overlay, however, which is much more recent and it is this I wish to try treat in detail.; partly because it is far better documented than previous layers, and partly because it seems to be a deeply interesting picture of human endeavour and "higher guidance". This overlay was crafted in the period from 1860 or so to the late 1930's. Some parts of it were definitely being worked on in the early 1970's and may even be still in the process of development.

To summarise the whole thing in a few words; it was an attempt by a loose group of people to use a powerful occult structure to transform the consciousness, the spirit, of their "race". The idea of race was very prevalent then, as were various speculations on spiritism, the Israelite origins of many European peoples and royal houses, and Celtic culture as a revivifying and unifying force. Druidry and Masonry were popular, social reform movements proliferated and were very influential. In Glastonbury all this began to crystallise into what is basically a magical "Engine", an empowered symbol built into the landscape to change the awareness of anyone attuned to it in any way. It seems to have been begun by John Arthur Goodchild and Wellesley Tudor Pole. Whether they secretly cooperated or not is unknown to me. Certainly, they knew of each other, but equally certainly, both were "talented" in various psychic perceptions. In 1898, Goodchild placed a glass bowl in Bride's Well at Beckery. With it he placed a ruby, a cross and a gold chain. He performed a ceremony there, after which he sent the remaining item, a glass platter, to a "son of Garibaldi" in Italy. He then left the bowl to be found by young maidens, as he had been instructed in a vision.

The full story of this episode, more or less, can be found in "*The Avalonians*" by Patrick Benham. In fact, this book is essential reading! Goodchild was basically a mystical Christian with esoteric leanings. He was a wealthy doctor and bachelor, who worked in Italy among the expatriate Britons convalescing there. He was well informed and literate, a capable author and poet. He would have been well aware of

51

the then recent unification of Italy under the influence of General Garibaldi, who used basic Masonic techniques to organise his push to unify the country and was for a time (the 1890's) the Grand Master of the Rite of Mizraim (an esoteric Egyptian-based Masonic system of ritual degrees). He would probably have been aware of the many Rosicrucian organisations in Europe. He may even have been a Rosicrucian him-self. I have no evidence.

Goodchild was certainly a champion of "spiritual womanhood" as a path to peace. He wrote a book about it, in which a colony of the Tribe of Dan reached Eire and lived well under the generous Great Queen (Mor Rigan). The enlightened teachings of this woman fused with early Christianity to form the cult of Brigit within the early Celtic Church. Over centuries this cult and its great Queen were deliberately buried in Roman Catholic propaganda to leave the Morrigan, a terrible and cruel War Goddess. He believed that the old ridge at Beckery where Bridget had left the bell and weaving gear was in fact a College of the Mysteries of Bride, where women carried the Great Queen's teaching on into the Christian world. He saw the ridge as the back of the "Salmon of Wisdom". The pool of Bride's Well was then perhaps the sacred pool in which it fed on the nut of wisdom?? However, there was no hazel here, only a thorn, the Faery Tree, and a stone above the culvert into the Brue. The Faery Tree is relevant, as one of Goodchild's greatest friends was William Sharpe, a capable faery seer, whose alter ego Fiona McLeod wrote much useful faery lore and may even "herself" have been the result of experimental work in faery/human communication. I say this because Sharpe was also friends with W.B. Yeats, whose connections with faery, with the Golden Dawn and with the politics of the Celtic Revival are well known and documented; and these documents refer to Sharpe's work on several occasions.

Sharpe knew of the bowl. He also renamed Wearyall Hill as "Uriel's Hill, Uriel the angel of the Sun", and revealed the curious "Triad" poem in the Abbey grounds. Both of these things are relevant as you will see.

Leaving Goodchild and Sharpe and the Bowl in its well, we move to Wellesley Tudor Pole. A young grain merchant of Bristol, Wellesley had a dream in 1902, in which he was a monk of Glastonbury. It was so clear that he went to check it out and was hooked. He was convinced a holy relic waited there to be found. He was also sure it should be found by three maidens, a "Triad". He set about finding and training a Triad, beginning with his sister Katherine, later adding the Allen sisters, friends of the family. He trained them by taking them around "an old pilgrimage route" at Glastonbury. They went round it many times, performing ceremonies at certain places, picnicking halfway, visiting the special "women's place" at Maidencroft, playing music and singing. Apparently they were tracing the form of the later magical "Engine" on the ground and empowering it with their visions and prayers and ceremonies – Katherine expressed a hope that they had made a good spiritual channel and thus she must have had some idea of what they were doing.

All the flow of power channelled by this work went into the Bowl in its well, empowering and attuning it to the image of Bride. This attunement was deeply refined when they found the Bowl, took news of it to Goodchild, whom they knew, and took it to Bristol where they set it up in an Oratory under Goodchild's guidance. This Oratory was unique. It was open to the public and was cared for by the Triad of Maidens, who used it for religious ceremonies, honouring Christ and Bride (and the moon…) and recorded all visitors and their visions in a diary. The diary still exists, as do their two Service books, and they are fascinating reading. There was also a picture of the Bowl. Painted by Goodchild, which carried upon it "The True Name and Number of the Christ" and the two symbols recording visions he had had of a sword and a cup, before the Bowl was found.

An interesting digression here: Goodchild was greatly interested in Gematria and the "True Name" adds up to the "True Number".

If the "True Number" is turned into Hebrew letters of the correct number values:

1=A; 6=V; 2=B; so the True Number spells A V D B

which is then reversed as Hebrew reads right to left giving B V D A

In early Brythonic, BODVA is crow or raven. We recall that the Morrigan is a triple goddess, her three names are Nemain (terror), Macha (the mare) and Badbh (crow). Badbh is BODVA in a later form.

The Christ is identified with the Crow aspect of the Morrigan – one wonders why? Was this an initially benevolent face of the Dannite Great Queen in Goodchild's vision?

THE GENERAL LAYOUT OF GOODCHILD'S
BOARD "REVEALING OPENLY THE TRUE
NAME AND NUMBER OF THE CHRIST"
IN THE ORATORY AT CLIFTON, BRISTOL.

So far, we have a pilgrimage "as a spiritual channel" and an empowered well and a more precisely attuned glass bowl relating to Bride, Christ and the Morrigan (and water, femininity and the Moon).

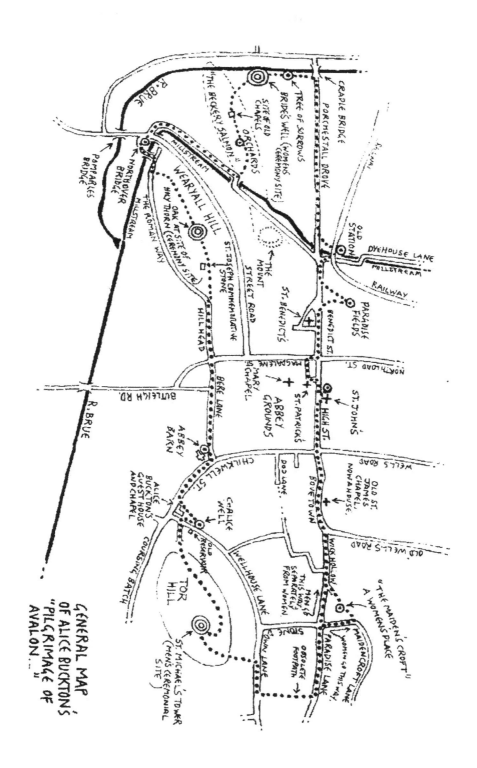

GENERAL MAP
OF ALICE BUCKTON'S
"PILGRIMAGE OF
AVALON..."

Now things start to get out of hand! Firstly, Alice Buckton hears of the now-famous Bowl and comes to meet its guardians in 1907. Alice is a London pioneer of primary education and a poet and playwright and is deeply into the idea of spiritual womanhood, especially as a prerequisite of sane children. She takes a liking to Glastonbury, wishing to set up a women's community there. She returns to London.

Wellesley is told by psychics that there are documents about the Bowl hidden in Constantinople, so he goes there to find them., but instead finds some Baha'i's and brings back their teachings to England. He contacts other Baha'i's in London (there were very few then) and gets involved in their ideas and organisation and Alice too becomes part of that organisation. Baha'i nowadays is a separate faith, with its own laws, institutions, etc., but in those days it was seen as a movement to propagate ideas, which would help rejuvenate the major faiths of the time. This was something Wellesley agreed was necessary, so he took part enthusiastically. When Abdul-Baha, the Baha'i founder's son came to the West in 1911, he came to visit the Oratory in Bristol. He picked up the Bowl, looked into it long, then blessed it; in fact, he blessed the whole house, saying it would in time become a resting place for pilgrims.

Both Alice and Wellesley kept up their contact with the Baha'i Movement and they also continued to pursue their previous goals. Wellesley kept up the search for documents in Constantinople for many years without success. He also did work to connect the Glastonbury setup to other sites. He, the Triad, his friend David Russell and others planned to "awaken the three Heart Centres of the British Isles". These were seen as early centres of Celtic Christian spirituality which needed to be opened up to attract pilgrims who would disseminate spiritual renewal countrywide. Wellesley's early sketch-map of this idea shows Iona, Glastonbury and a point somewhere in the mouth of the Shannon river – my guess is Scattery Island monastery. However, this changed later (maybe when southern Ireland separated from Great Britain) to an island called Devenish in Lough Erne (Co. Fermanagh). David Russell helped push for the opening up of Iona – the Triad went on pilgrimage around it, opening up sites with the Bowl's energies.

Then Devenish was approached, but nothing worked: Devenish repelled all attempts to open it.

Meanwhile Alice had bought the old Catholic Seminary at Chalice Well in 1913 and turned it into a guest house and school of arts and crafts. She beat Rutland Boughton and Philip Oyler to the post, pushed into buying the place by Archdeacon Wilberforce of Westminster. Why is not clear. It is possible that Wilberforce was heading off Wellesley Tudor Pole, whose supposed "Grail cup" had taken him in somewhat and caused some embarrassment.

Philip Oyler may have got Wellesley's help in sorting out the purchase of the Well, perhaps with the idea of the Bowl going there along with Boughton's Opera School and Oyler's organic farm. Sources are unclear on this. Certainly, Philip Oyler and Wellesley seem to have stayed in touch right into Oyler's old age in France. He was always a competent champion of sustainable farming methods and his books are worth seeking out.

The Pilgrimage route now comes into its own. Alice inherited it from the Triad of Maidens. She took her guests around it and wrote it all down for Miss Felicity Hardcastle in the 1920's. The description of it was published in the Chalice Well Messenger of 1998 and it is worth reading in full. It gives much detail as to the structure underlying the pilgrimage and contains several interesting references, notably to King Arthur, Bride, various archangels and to "the Watchers": in fact "the Watchers" are central to its structure. "Watchers" are obviously spirit beings, though it is unclear exactly what kind of spirits they are. They seek people to do their work in the world, they pass on the mysteries to those who come to meet them at their Thorn. The archangels "watch over" various levels at Glastonbury.

Watchers are also the fearsome fallen angels in the Book of Enoch (a book popular in Masonic circles as Enoch features in some Masonic histories). Frederick Bligh Bond, the excavator of Glastonbury Abbey in the early years of Alice's life at Glastonbury, also knew of the Watchers – this was one of the titles of the group of spirits who dictated to him (via automatic writing through several hands) many secrets and tales and hints as to where to dig next. Were the Watchers a part of the 1902 pilgrimage or did Alice put them in after hearing Bligh Bond describe them? She and Bligh Bond were friends and swapped things. She gave him a poem, he designed a wrought iron well cover for her – it is still there. They may have shared much knowledge, we have little evidence so far. Certainly, knowledge was to be had. Alice's first play at Glastonbury was "The Coming of Bride". This is an expansion of a book by Fiona McLeod about Bride on Iona. It adds a section where Bride comes to Glastonbury and is welcomed by druids (who are portrayed in interesting detail). The play was collectively written and the cast included one of the Triad of Maidens.

Maybe Goodchild's words were there somewhere – he died in 1914, the year of the play's production.

From Alice's Pilgrimage we can deduce much of the structure of this magical Engine, but one thing is missing. What symbol stood in the North? What image can suggest both the highest spirit and most basic earth in one form? Bligh Bond turned out to have the answer. Scripts sent to him in 1928 from America and published locally as "The Glastonbury Scripts" give a series of poetic tales of Joseph of Arimathea and his bringing of the Sangreal, "the holy blood and water" to Glastonbury in the form of a stone, "a white beryl with a rosy tint at its heart". This stone was known as "the Rose" and called "She". Here is our Northern station symbol then, a stone rose.

Now we have a complete set of Glastonbury Hallows at least one of which exists as a physical object – the Bowl. I wonder if any of the others exist anywhere? If so, why are they not as visible as the Bowl?

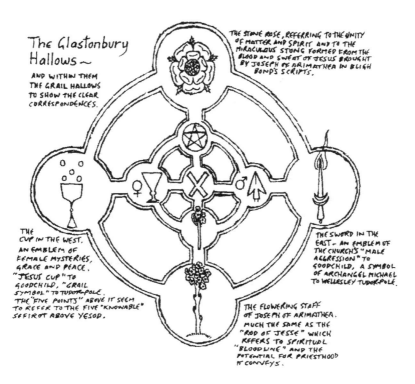

**The Glastonbury Hallows ~**

AND WITHIN THEM THE GRAIL HALLOWS TO SHOW THE CLEAR CORRESPONDENCES.

THE STONE ROSE, REFERRING TO THE UNITY OF MATTER AND SPIRIT AND TO THE MIRACULOUS STONE FORMED FROM THE BLOOD AND SWEAT OF JESUS BROUGHT BY JOSEPH OF ARIMATHEA IN BLIGH BOND'S SCRIPTS.

THE CUP IN THE WEST, AN EMBLEM OF FEMALE MYSTERIES, GRACE AND PEACE, "JESUS CUP" TO GOODCHILD, "GRAIL SYMBOL" TO TUDOR-POLE. THE "FIVE POINTS" ABOVE IT SEEM TO REFER TO THE FIVE "KNOWABLE" SEFIROT ABOVE YESOD.

THE SWORD IN THE EAST ~ AN EMBLEM OF THE CHURCH'S "MALE AGGRESSION" TO GOODCHILD, A SYMBOL OF ARCHANGEL MICHAEL TO WELLESLEY TUDOR-POLE.

THE FLOWERING STAFF OF JOSEPH OF ARIMATHEA. MUCH THE SAME AS THE "ROD OF JESSE" WHICH REFERS TO SPIRITUAL "BLOODLINE" AND THE POTENTIAL FOR PRIESTHOOD IT CONVEYS.

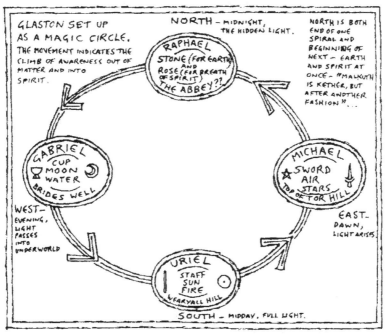

GLASTON SET UP AS A MAGIC CIRCLE. THE MOVEMENT INDICATES THE CLIMB OF AWARENESS OUT OF MATTER AND INTO SPIRIT.

NORTH ~ MIDNIGHT, THE HIDDEN LIGHT.

NORTH IS BOTH END OF ONE SPIRAL AND BEGINNING OF NEXT ~ EARTH AND SPIRIT AT ONCE ~ "MALKUTH IS KETHER, BUT AFTER ANOTHER FASHION"...

RAPHAEL
STONE (FOR EARTH AND ROSE (FOR BREATH OF SPIRIT)
THE ABBEY ??

GABRIEL
CUP MOON WATER
BRIDES WELL

MICHAEL
SWORD AIR STARS
TOP OF TOR HILL

URIEL
STAFF SUN FIRE
WEARYALL HILL

WEST ~ EVENING, LIGHT PASSES INTO UNDERWORLD

EAST ~ DAWN, LIGHT ARISES.

SOUTH ~ MIDDAY, FULL LIGHT.

We also have another clue – "Sangreal". The Sangreal bloodline of the Magdalene is topical now and many books have been written about it. The "Bloodline of the Grail" praises Margaret Starbird for getting the Tarot right in terms of its connection with Grail lore. The suits of the Tarot are the "Grail Hallows". They are also a pretty close match with our "Glastonbury Hallows". Was the intent of this local overlay to produce some kind of magically empowered exposition of the Grail? It is hard to say as the structure seems to have drifted off balance and never quite been completed.

Bond worked to tie the Abbey into a system of sacred number and geometry and to link it with the Old Church and Joseph of Arimathea's foundation.

Wellesley Tudor Pole continued to work with the pilgrimages on Iona and Glastonbury with an "Order of St. Michael" more or less up to his death. There are several relics of this order in existence. One is a wooden wheel displaying a ribbon on which Margaret Thornley's many visits to "Michael" sites are recorded. Wellesley and Katherine Tudor Pole and the Bowl were at her service in her work of awakening old Michael centres to the light. This all seem to have been part of a process of helping the changeover from Gabriel's rulership of the Piscean Age to Michael's rulership of the Aquarian Age, an idea arising from Rudolf Steiner's work. There are even articles in old *"Messenger of Chalice Well" magazines (nos 35, 36 & 37)* which describe the three island "Heart Centres" in detail. Obviously this work was continuing in 1978/9 …

There is a link to Iona which seems to reflect the basic dynamic structure of the Pilgrimage at Glastonbury: a cup at one end, a sword at the other. The cup was the one from Bride's Well, the sword was a wooden sculpture of the Sword of St. Michael subduing the dragon, commissioned by Wellesley in the 1950's, sent to Iona in the 1960's and set up in the south of the Michael chapel there, broken up by persons unknown and sent back, minus sword to Chalice Well at a later date… A curious tale. Even more curious is a similar link implied by Goodchild sending away the platter to Italy. If we imagine a sequence of Cup–Platter-Sword in which the cup is at Bride's Well, the platter is a "sun disc", meaning much the same as the solar "rod" at Wearyall, and the sword is the point at which stellar energies or divine power enters the knowable worlds at Da'ath as on the Tor. We can posit a connection between the world to reach Egypt. If the line passes through Venice, it ends near Cairo (Giza Plateau?) Egypt as a spiritual source, mediated through Italy and collected in the Bowl in Glastonbury.

This gives us empowerment from Iona (via the Isle of Man as mediating "solar station") to Beckery, carrying early Celtic/Druidic Brigit spirituality. And empowerment from Egypt carrying Hermetic mysteries and the influence of early Coptic Christianity (mediated by Italian Masonry??). A fascinating mixture, which is present quite strongly in Glastonbury even now.

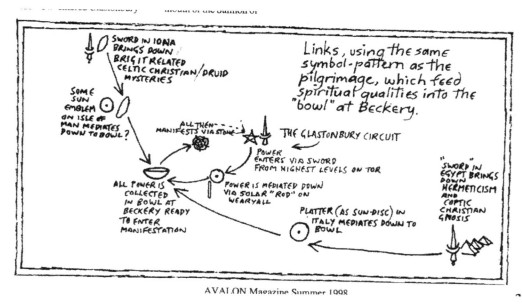

There is a feeling that all of this effort was in preparation in some way for the changing of the Age. A means to feed into the deep mind of the Race ideas which would make it easier to let go of Piscean ideals and assimilate Aquarian ones. Wellesley's Order of St. Michael seemed to serve this purpose. Chalice Well sits at the mouth of Katherine Maltwood's "Aquarian Phoenix" and is thus the "point of utterance" of the coming age. Alice Buckton wrote a poem "Rune of the Waterbearer"

which speaks of the change of Age; Dion Fortune set up her own school in Chalice Orchard (also the Phoenix's mouth) and worked through the Second World War to defend Britain and prepare for the coming Age. And of course the Blue Bowl entered Glastonbury in the mouth of the Salmon of Wisdom (Pisces). Rested in the care of Katherine Tudor Pole for many years and was put by Wellesley where he thought it should be in the Aquarian Phoenix's mouth at Chalice Well.

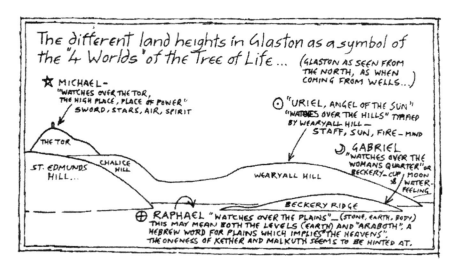

The different land heights in Glaston as a symbol of the "4 Worlds" of the Tree of Life... (GLASTON AS SEEN FROM THE NORTH, AS WHEN COMING FROM WELLS...)

☆ MICHAEL—
"WATCHES OVER THE TOR, THE HIGH PLACE, PLACE OF POWER" SWORD, STARS, AIR, SPIRIT

THE TOR

ST. EDMUNDS HILL... CHALICE HILL

☉ "URIEL, ANGEL OF THE SUN" "WATCHES OVER THE HILLS" TYPIFIED BY WEARYALL HILL— STAFF, SUN, FIRE—MIND

☽ GABRIEL "WATCHES OVER THE WOMANS QUARTER" OR BECKERY—CUP, MOON ☆ WATER—FEELING

WEARYALL HILL

BECKERY RIDGE

⊕ RAPHAEL "WATCHES OVER THE PLAINS"—(STONE, EARTH, BODY) THIS MAY MEAN BOTH THE LEVELS (EARTH) AND "ARABOTH", A HEBREW WORD FOR PLAINS WHICH IMPLIES "THE HEAVENS". THE ONENESS OF KETHER AND MALKUTH SEEMS TO BE HINTED AT.

Interesting as all this is, it is in no way a complete picture. New evidence arises daily, each item modifying the whole somewhat. Also, there are curious loose ends. Why was Bligh Bond so interested in the Loretto chapel? This is a chapel of Italian design set up by Abbot Bere after his ambassadorial work in Italy, part of a network of pilgrim sites related to a copy of Mary's House set up (in Loretto, Italy) after a vision and having its own special litany, a sequence of titles of Mary resembling the long recitations of Goddess titles common in Roman paganism.

Another loose link: Felicity Hardcastle, the author of Chalice Well's History, amateur archaeologist, helper of Bligh Bond when he excavated the Loretto chapel, friend of Alice Buckton and the Triad of Maidens, early helper of the present Chalice Well Trust and probably a member of Wellesley Tudor Pole's "Order of St. Michael" is present in some way throughout the whole tale but very little is known of her.

## ∴ THE PILGRIMAGE UPON THE COMPOSITE TREE OF LIFE ∴

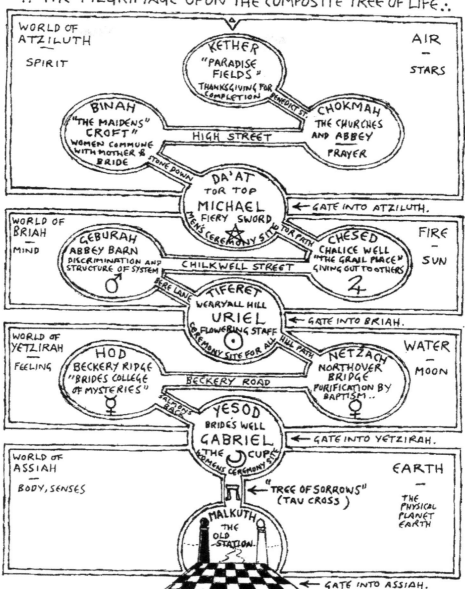

The pilgrimage climbs the tree along the "lightning flash".
Some of the Archangel's positions on the Middle Pillar are
odd, but they fit both Alice Buckton's and Goodchild's material.

There is far more work to do on all of this and it needs to be done by better scholars than I. All I can say is that Glastonbury has myths which are wonderful in their own way and it has a history, which I hope I have shown is even more wonderful than many of the myths. May hearts and minds be opened, there so much more to be found.

*Avalon Magazine, Issue 9, Summer 1998*

# ST. JOSEPH'S WELL AND THE PASSAGE TO THE TOR

**Alan Royce** *checks out the myths around this ancient well, and finds that the reality may be more exciting than the fiction.*

Anyone familiar with Glastonbury Abbey will have heard of St. Joseph's Well. They may also be familiar with the story behind it. The most common version of this tale says that the well was dedicated to St. Joseph of Arimathea long ago (perhaps it was the well beside his little wattle church; perhaps the monks dedicated it later in order to give a focus for pilgrims visiting St. Joseph's chapel), but was lost when the abbey was 'dissolved' in 1539. For many years the abbey was a 'picturesque ruin' in mainly agricultural use in the middle of a slowly recovering Glastonbury, and the crypt below St. Joseph's (or is it St. Mary's?) chapel, obscured by rubble and weeds, was not even thought worthy of mention by 17th century chroniclers.

In 1825 the well was uncovered "by a party of gentlemen, in searching for hidden Antiquities". These gentlemen decided that the well was a Holy Well and was used by the monks "in aid of their miracles". The contemporary Roman Catholic believers, consulted on the subject, disagreed, saying it was a place for washing vestments and the like. The story stuck, however, and the well became a Holy Well of St. Joseph – a place where pilgrims had taken the Holy Waters while visiting Joseph's shrine.

This story, with embellishments, is still believed today. But was it really so?

I have found the well fascinating since my first visit to Glastonbury in the very early 1970s, but it is only recently that I have made any serious attempt to look into it (sorry for the pun).

I was quite happy with the story at first. The abbey seems to have adopted the St. Joseph story (and other useful bits of the Grail Mythos) around 1250 or so, and put it all to good use both financially and as an esoteric deepening of contemplative Christian life in the area. This process seems to have expanded slowly over the years, and really seems to have taken off around 1450 or so, not long after which the crypt was built.

However, on careful inspection of the crypt and well, and its curious chamber and stairways, I began to wonder. Not being a brilliant architectural historian, I decided to consult one. A certain Professor Willis wrote a serious survey of the then known parts of the abbey around 1865, and he says some very interesting things.

Apparently, before the crypt was properly cleaned out in the 1820s, the top of the doorway leading to the well chamber was visible, and the local folk had a strong belief that it was the start of an underground passage leading to the Tor, St. Michael's Hill. Willis pooh-poohs the "recent romanticising" about the well-being connected to Joseph of Arimathea's cult. He repeats the story that "Romanists" claimed the well was a simple place for washing vestments, and that there was a vestry above it linked to the Mary Chapel.

Willis was of the opinion that the crypt was opened in two phases. The two bays to the east of the chapel were dug first, somewhere around 1500. This was simply achieved by digging out the soil between the foundation walls of the Galilee, reusing old Norman stonework to construct the vaulting (either for antique effect or because it was available ready cut) and cutting side alcoves for windows and (probably) stairs down for access. The Galilee above would have been taken out of use during construction and restored afterwards.

Willis felt this crypt was purely utilitarian, and related to the custom of storing the bodies of those who could afford the privilege as near as possible to St. Joseph's shrine (which seems to be in much the same location as Mary's chapel). Certainly, when the crypt was cleared, it was found to be full of rubble, water and many jumbled lead coffins. Little space for a shrine there.

Somewhere around the early 1300s, the east wall of the Mary Chapel was removed (down to the floor level, leaving the foundation wall below in place) to allow full access from the Galilee. The stonework was saved, as we shall see.

This would have allowed the chapel altars etc. to be freely moved, as the crypt construction rendered areas unusable for a time.

*The first phase of the crypt dug in 1500   at least, as I understand it*

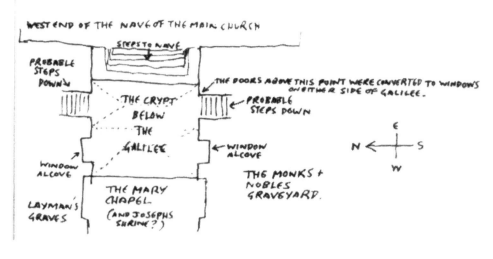

*The second phase of the crypt, below the Mary chapel*

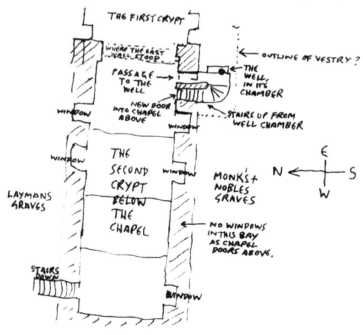

The second stage of the crypt was begun a few years after 1500, when the demand for coffin storage seems to have escalated. The Mary chapel was closed, and its function moved into the Galilee. The floor was removed, the soil below removed, the east foundation wall removed, and the other walls pierced to make window alcoves, a new stair access in the north-west corner, a passage to the well and its chamber, and a new doorway in the south wall of the chapel above. All was faced in new stonework, and new vaulting was constructed. The floor was replaced at a higher level. A stair was added from the well to the small new chapel door, and the 'vestry' was added or enlarged (you can see its roof line cut into the south wall of the chapel).

The well itself if interesting. It seems to have been covered with an arch made up of components salvaged from the window-heads of the deleted east wall of the Mary chapel. You can see their siblings still *in situ* in the remaining chapel windows.

*The general appearance of the well in its arch of window parts*

This well arch could have been put in place any time between, say, 1320 and 1520, and the well's age becomes of relevance here. At one extreme, the well could, indeed, be a Roman well of Joseph's time. At the other extreme, it could all have been constructed out of recycled parts in the 1500s, as part of one functional space relating to the work with bodies and their storage.

Firstly I wondered what its story might have been if it were, in truth, a Roman well. The most obvious issue was its level: the present mouth of the well is, more or less, at Roman ground level. The wooden 'Old Church' mentioned as the original focus of the abbey would have stood at this level, and the well could have been found near its south-east corner (if indeed it had corners and was not round as some suggest).

This state of affairs probably continued through the Irish/British phase of the monastery, and perhaps into the Saxon abbey of the 800s. In Dunstan's time, however (990 or so), the level of the graveyard was raised a full ten feet or more to allow another 'storey' of burials. As the 'Old Church' was obviously not buried by this process, some kind of bank or retaining wall must have separated it from the new cemetery. One can imagine the well being included with the church, simply to save the work of relining it.

Later, the 'Old Church' was sheathed in lead to preserve and (if my memory is correct) covered entirely by a new chapel. This would allow the cemetery to expand to the chapel's walls, and only the well and the chapel interior would remain at the old level. The well would now need steps for access.

It is strange to imagine the tiny 'Old Church" sitting, in effect, in its own crypt up until the great fire (1184?), when all was reduced to ashes!

The 1200s saw the slow reconstruction of the site and the erection of the present chapel – its foundation walls presumably built in the convenient pit which was all that remained of previous structures. The central void was filled with soil up to the general ground level, there being no reason left to do otherwise. Our conjectural well chamber by now might be roofed over, but would still be extant.

It is interesting to think that, when you stand in the present crypt, you may well be within the actual space occupied by the 'Old Wooden Church' so long ago!

The 'Old Church  and its possible well

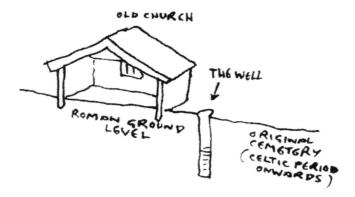

The 'Old Church  and well, circa 990

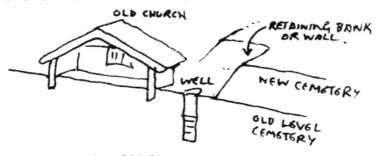

The 'Old Church   the well in its pit,
and the new chapel, 1100s

Now, let us return to the "Passage to the Tor".

The next author I consulted was Frederick Bligh Bond, the first real excavator of the abbey from 1907 until his dismissal in 1922. Bond says much about the well. He relates an old story which claims that a passage arising from the south wall of the well chamber was in-filled by the farmer about fifty years before his time "because the lambs kept falling into it". Bond tested this idea by digging around the chamber wall, and did indeed find evidence of a deep trench, in the right place, which had been in-filled with clay – quite distinguishable from the general rubble of the graveyard. The lack of passage walling might simply suggest that the good building stone had been 'robbed out' before filling the hold, but Bond was still not a hundred percent convinced by the passage story. I was intrigued by Bond's story for reasons I will explain later. But on with the tour!

Bond was not certain of the age of the well, either, but he seems to have been in sympathy with the idea that the crypt was a place of pilgrimage in the St. Joseph cult. (Actually, Bond was very interested in the Joseph cult, but for complex reasons of his own which are another story.) He cites the many holes in the early crypt vaulting which could have supported many hanging lanterns – something needed lots of light down there. He also calls attention to the probable form of the stairs into the well chamber. In the present chamber there are five steps to a spiral Newel Stair, which terminate in a platform around hip height. A curious 'Ladder Stair', considered modern by Willis and Bond, leads up to the chapel doorway (look down through the floor grill outside the door).

Bond believed the Newel Stair continued around originally to a junction point (you can see the chisel marks where the steps were cut flush with the wall above the platform). At this junction, the stair divided into a branch to the small chapel door, and a larger branch which ran above the crypt passage and along the side of the outer chapel wall to a door into the Galilee. You can see some step-ends cut into the wall basement blocks in just the right place to the right of the small chapel door, outside.

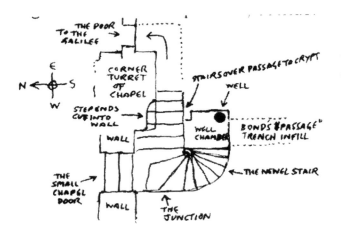

*How the Newel Stair probably looked when in use*

All this could have been made in one go (circa 1500), or the passage to the crypt and the stair to the chapel could have been added to an already old set-up dating from circa 1300. (The wall basement itself is 13th century, the well arch not earlier than 14th century.) The passage going south, if real, could be of almost any date.

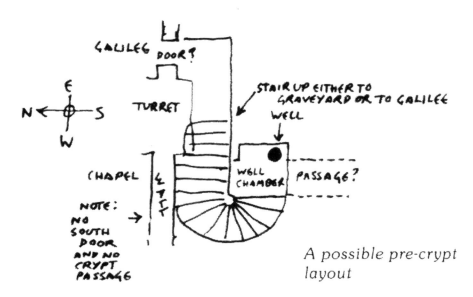

*A possible pre-crypt layout*

The 'Ladder Stair' and the current roof vault of the well chamber are both probably of the 1800s – repairs to the robbing out and general mayhem of the Dissolution.

All this is interesting, but none of it rules out an early well which has undergone modification and repair. However, Bond says more – he also claims that the well is not a true well but is fed from a conduit (which he found in the south-east corner of the crypt) which "carried in water from further up the hill". He then goes on to describe a larger conduit from Chalice Well to the abbey site, and many have misread this to mean that the "St. Joseph" well is fed from the same source as Chalice Well.

Thus far, the well seems to be a convenient cavity, artificially placed and fed, as a place to fill buckets when at work in crypt or chapel. This suggests a late date and a purely functional use, as Willis suggests, so now I will confuse things further by describing the reason for my interest in Bond's passage.

A year or so back, as part of a visionary working led by someone who wished us to connect with the spirit of the abbey when it was still in use, I found myself (in vision, of course) standing in the little well chamber in the company of a 13th century monastic, probably a lay brother, who showed me how he and his friends used the well in their spiritual practice. This involved kneeling by the well with a single lamp, reading from a very homemade-looking vellum psalter (or the like), contemplating the 'death and rebirth' of Christ in the tomb of St. Joseph, and applying the spirit of this contemplation to their own state as 'tombs of spirit' in the hope of Christ's rebirth occurring in their own hearts.

Apart from this lesson in mediaeval spirituality, the chap also showed me the stone passage which led south from the well and had stone shelves full of skulls and various long bones – relics related in some way to their physical and spiritual work. Perhaps this will make clear my interest in Bond's passage. But there is more to come.

Bond also writes about the discovery of the foundations of St. Michael's chapel in the middle of the old cemetery – a structure rebuilt in 1300 or so as it was then in decay. He found this due south of the well, about halfway between the crypt and the Abbot's Halls. It, too, seems to have had some kind of crypt "filled up with compacted bone", a friend tells me. This caused me to speculate on the possible symbolic pattern involved in all this, hinted at in my visionary encounter. I write this down in the hope that someone may find it useful.

Imagine that the passage in my vision linked the well-chamber to the bone store below the Michael chapel. This allows a guess at how the mortuary work in the abbey might have been ritualised, or made sacred, in the context of these chambers. 'Joseph', both as Jesus's father and his alleged uncle Joseph of Arimathea, symbolises a power which makes a tomb for Jesus (one a body as tomb for his spirit, the other a cave as tomb for his body). The first Joseph supervises Jesus's entry into the 'cave' of this world; the second Joseph facilitates his exit from the cave of this world as a resurrected spirit.

This mysterious process of dying to the inheritance of the body and being reborn to the inheritance of the Holy Spirit, of dying to self-will and being reborn as an expression of the will of Christ within, was basic to the more serious, initiated Christians of the Early Church, and was perfectly suited to being celebrated in a sepulchral context. The importance of relics, especially bones, as a contactable residue of the essence or spirit of a saintly person, is also relevant.

The passage, if real, would have linked a place where the 'Joseph' death and rebirth mystery could be celebrated to a place where the 'Michael' mystery might be performed – wherein the essence (as bones) was placed under the care and guidance of the Archangel Michael, as the great psychopomp of Christian symbolism.

It is worth saying here that the Michael chapel was also dedicated to the Saints in general, especially Joseph of Arimathea. Was this the source of the name later applied to the Mary chapel?

Of course, both Josephs are linked to a Mary. The name "Mary" provides another generic term for a function. These 'Marys' seem to symbolise two modes of Birthing – one at each end of Jesus's life. Mary the Virgo bore Jesus's body into the cave; Mary of Magdala, by her unique perceptiveness, bore his spirit out of the cave and into limitless realms. The first Mary sits in the east above Joseph's crypt and well; the second Mary is located (by John of Glastonbury) in the west at Beckery, Bridget's old chapel site. It is interesting that Bridget is "Bride" at Beckery; the Magdalene as fallen Sophia being rescued by her 'marriage' to the spirit as Jesus. John Arthur Goodchild made much of this around 1900.

*The layout of the Joseph and Michael chapels as a north-south polarity*

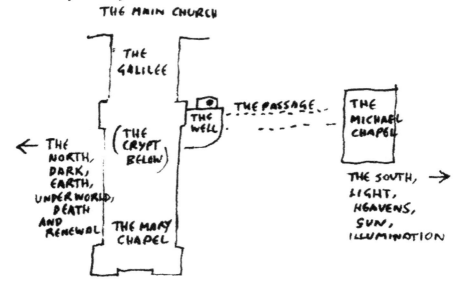

*The two Marys as an east-west polarity*

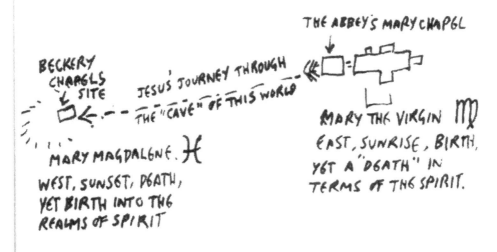

In my vision, the lay brothers' rite had elements of intercession for the souls of those entombed – this being understood to include the 'dead' soul of the one conducting the rite. This 'dead self' is alluded to in Jesus's quote, "let the dead bury their dead". The intention was to open a way to the heavens for all souls concerned, God willing.

This vision of mine is of course subjective, and hardly scientific evidence. But it triggers the idea that some kind of cult of salvatory effectiveness around the person of Joseph would help explain the sudden demand for all that coffin storage space. Also, the use of vision and myth as spiritual tools, combined with the presence of venerable relics and ancient buildings, is quite in sympathy with mediaeval practice. It is how educated pilgrims would have interacted with the place. I suspect these methods, applied as devotional tools, and tempered with wisdom, could still be of great value for those whose allegiance is to Christ when they visit the abbey.

My own interest is more in the long-term process of transmutation, whereby the ancient faiths of this area were sculpted by various divine revelations into the present state of affairs (not as dire as some believe). This is not a speedy process – you must live with a place for some time, and convince the spirits of place that your interest and sympathy are genuine, before any real unfolding will take place. That being said, may this trail of words suggest interesting places for you to go, and may your pilgrimage be truly blessed!

*Avalon Magazine, Issue 22, Autumn/Winter 2002*

# THE JOSEPH CHAPEL

**Alan Royce** *summarises his recent research
into one of the Glastonbury chapels.*

Back along, I wrote about the famous St Joseph's Well in Glastonbury Abbey, in which I looked at its form and history and put in a few of my own strange speculations as to its mythical background. Since that article, several new pieces of information have come to light, such as the true location of the old Michael chapel with its ossuary crypt, and some useful hints as to the true meaning of the tales of Joseph and the Magdalene and the two cruets.

In pursuit of the latter, we came upon the statement that, "The two cruets should be contemplated as the two children of the Magdalene", and that this was "part of the secret way of working with the powers of Glastonbury". This intriguing information led to an interest in the properties of the Vesica Piscis, as the name of "the Magdalene" in Greek is directly related to that august figure:

The ancient shorthand for the Vesica's internal proportions is 153:265, thus:

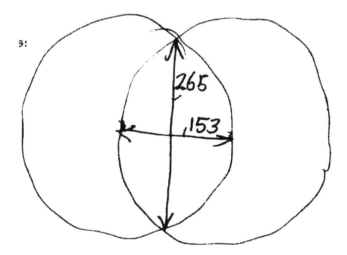

Now, the Vesica is the 'mother of all forms', by which is meant the regular polygons and their inherent irrational proportions etc.

Now, the Vesica is the 'mother of all forms', by which is meant the regular polygons and their inherent irrational proportions (√2 √3 √5) etc.
This idea can be developed into Pythagorean number, thus:

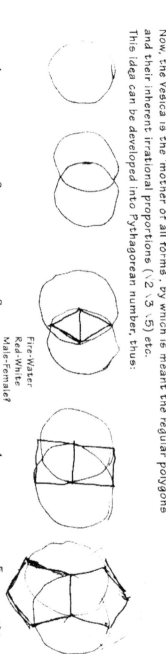

Fire-Water
Red-White
Male-Female?

| 1 | 2 | 3 | 4 | 5 |
|---|---|---|---|---|
| | | | | ... etc. |

The Source,
"Father"

The Dyad, The Other,
"Mother"

The (2) Children,
The Union of the Parents
3 = 2+1

The Elements,
The Mutual Reflections
of The One

The Divine Breath,
The First Motion

This idea can be developed into Pythagorean number and into an allegory of the Magdalene as the basic seed out of which the Christian Ecclesia unfolds. Mary is the one who perceives the nature of the risen Christ and conveys this Gnosis to others, who were fixated on his recent death until she opened their hearts.

We found that this unfolding of polygons seemed to be the basis of the iron well-cover put on Chalice Well in 1919. Bligh Bond seems to have had much to do with the design of this lid, and the hint is that it reflected his work at the Abbey, particularly his study of the measures of the Mary chapel. We tried the Vesica forms as overlays on both structures (you will perhaps note that the fit is a wee bit more convincing on the well than on the old chapel).

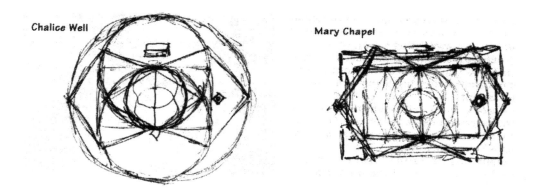

The two pentagons, or pentalphas, are the skeleton of the "Tudor Rose".

It would have been nice if the two roses had been the seed-form for the chapel – the Abbey abounds with double (and triple) roses and their related eight-fold containers. However, the fit is not good enough. It is always gratifying when a theory, but this one really did not. So what was really going on with this chapel?

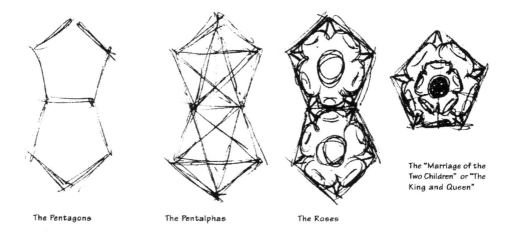

The Pentagons

The Pentalphas

The Roses

The "Marriage of the Two Children" or "The King and Queen"

(This 'five and eight' thing is mostly about the five retrogrades which the planet Venus executes in any eight-year period.)

A wise old serpent once told me, having been consulted about another Glastonbury legend, that I "should not bother about the stories, just pay close attention to the evidence". I applied this to the task in hand – forget Joseph and the Magdalene, forget roses, what is actually there?

Professor Willis' fine account of the 1860s Abbey ruins helped here, and the IESVS-MARIA stone on the chapel's south wall proved to be a major key.

You may have heard of Gematria, the use of the number value of the letters of ancient alphabets to convey meaning, as in the previous reference to 'H MAGDALENE =153'

This is mostly done in Hebrew and Greek, but the Latin script also had its gematria. Here are the letter values:

| A | B | C | D | E | F | G | H | I | L |
|---|---|---|---|---|---|---|---|---|---|
| 1 | 2 | 3 | 4 | 5 | 6 | 7 | 8 | 9 | 10 |

| M | N | O | P | Q | R | S | T | V | X |
|---|---|---|---|---|---|---|---|---|---|
| 11 | 12 | 13 | 14 | 15 | 16 | 17 | 18 | 19 | 20 |

...so the numbers on the stone are:

Which is interesting, as these numbers are in fact the two major dimensions of the building.

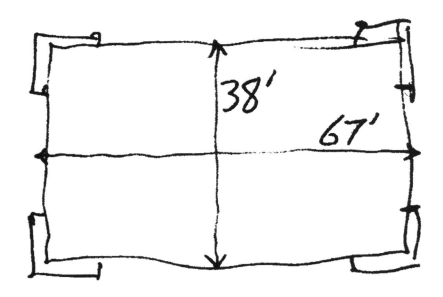

But it doesn't end here.

        38 x 4 = 152.    152 inches = 12 feet 8 inches.
        67 x 4 = 268.    268 inches = 22 feet 4 inches.

These dimensions are represented in the interior space of the chapel.

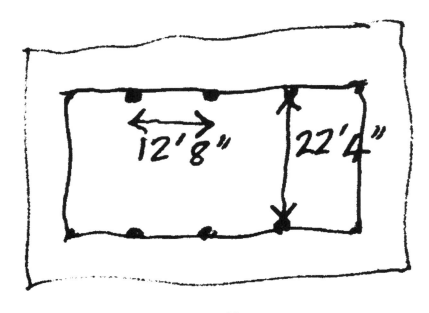

Now, 152 is the number of MIRIAM in Greek.

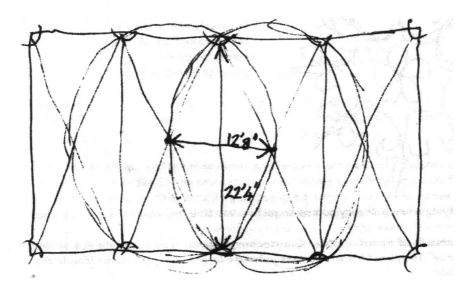

These dimensions are also Vesica numbers; the 152:268 Vesica, as opposed to the 153:265 Vesica of antiquity.

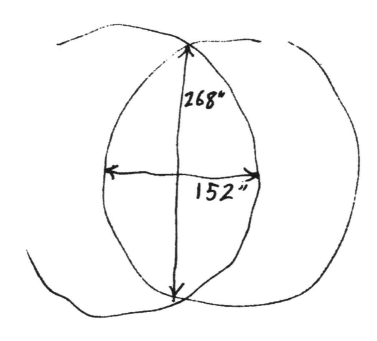

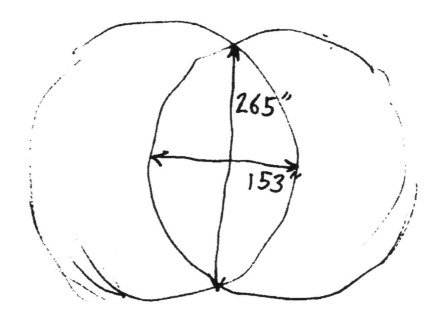

The original dimensions of the building can be reclaimed thus:

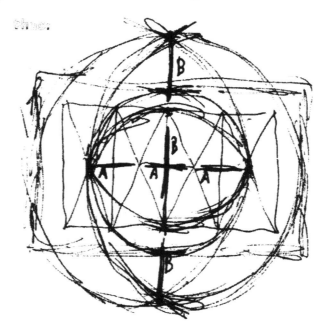

3 x 12 feet 8 inches = 38 feet
3 x 22 feet 4 inches = 67 feet.

Another useful way to look at the building is that used by Bligh Bond in his 'Mystery At Glaston':

12 feet 8 inches x 5 = 63 feet 4 inches
7 feet 5 1/3 inches x 5 = 37 feet 2 2/3 inches.

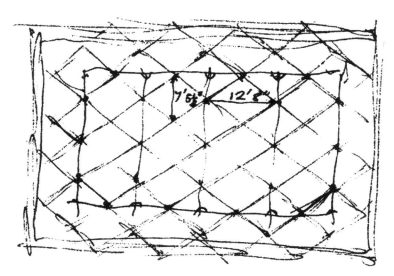

Bligh Bond's ideas depended on the relationship 37 feet : 64 feet being a Vesica relationship and an example of the connection between old English and Egyptian measures. He wished to demonstrate the Levantine origins of ancient Druidic culture, and the later development of same after Joseph of Arimathea's arrival. His "Glastonbury Scripts" are a major (channelled) source for the esoteric/alchemical Joseph tradition developed here between 1900 and the 1950s.

My own feeling is that the numbers derived from the IESVS MARIA stone describe the Mary chapel's symbolic dimensions somewhat better than Bligh Bond's ideas. though a great debt is still owed to him for the basic principles involved and for much of the background work!

Another layer to this can be glimpsed if the two names on the stone are permuted, in good gematric manner.

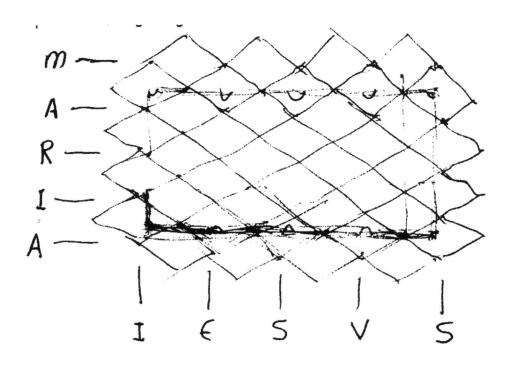

Or, more elegantly, as a 5 x 5 grid:

|  | 9<br>I | 5<br>E | 17<br>S | 19<br>V | 17<br>S |
|---|---|---|---|---|---|
| 11 m | 20 | 6 | 28 | 30 | 28 |
| 1 A | 0 | 6 | 18 | 20 | 18 |
| 16 R | 25 | 21 | 33 | 35 | 33 |
| 9 I | 18 | 14 | 26 | 28 | 26 |
| 1 A | 10 | 6 | 18 | 20 | 18 |

The letter numbers can be summed at each junction to reveal curious patterns, which do in fact relate to the building's form and purpose.

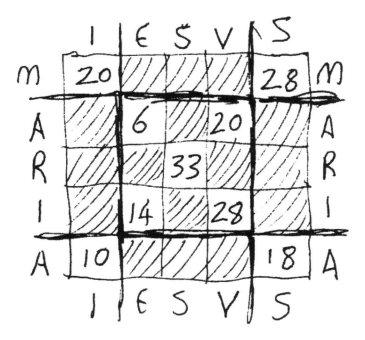

IESVS is contained in the body of MARIA. Also, the letters themselves make interesting words:

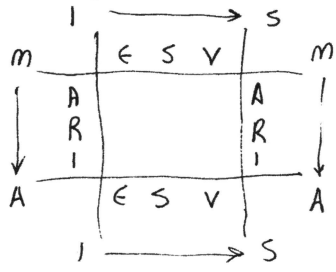

IS (ISH) is 'man' in Hebrew. A(m)MA is 'mother'. AM is an Irish word, which Goodchild considered a name of God. ESV (ESHV) is Jesus' name in Aramaic/Hebrew. ARI is 'lion' in Hebrew (Lion of Judah?).

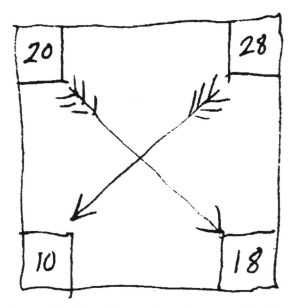

Shell of building: add either diagonal and you get the MARIA number =38.

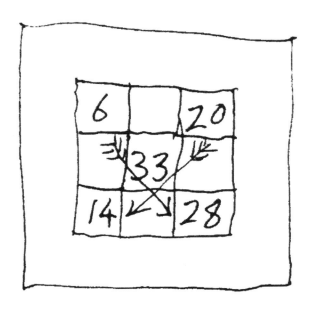

Interior of building: add either diagonal and you get the IESVS number = 67

The truly obsessive amongst you may freely play with the numbers and letters to find all sorts of monkish entertainment!

Now, the more devious side of me wonders if the perfectly conventional 152 = Mary the Blessed Virgin might conceal the 153 = Mary the Magdalene. Only a careful study of the actual measures would confirm or disprove this. Our 12 feet 8 inches would become 12 feet 9 inches, and our 22 feet 4 inches would become 22 feet 1 inch (perhaps, as 265 rather than 268). In case anyone wants to check these things out, this gives:

> 12 feet 9 inches x 3 = 38 feet 3 inches
> 12 feet 9 inches x 5 = 63 feet 9 inches
>
> 22 feet 1inch x 3 = 66 feet 3 inches
> 7 feet 4 1/3 inches x 5 = 36 feet 9 2/3 inches

Given the small differences, and the distressed and time-distorted state of the chapel, this could be a difficult exercise!

I hope this little ramble gives a few ideas for the further investigation of Glastonbury's deep and varied heritage. To know the intent of the old monks, it helps to try to look through their eyes.

*Avalon Magazine Issue 26, Spring 2004*

# DION FORTUNE & THE AVALONIAN TRADITION

**Alan Royce** *sets the Glastonbury work of Dion*
*Fortune into its historical and mythical context.*

Anyone who has scratched below the surface of modern Goddess spirituality is likely to have heard of Dion Fortune. A little more delving, and they may have discovered Dion's connection to Glastonbury and its area, her "Avalon of the Heart".

Dion Fortune is rightly credited with many powerful innovations which are the basis of much modern esoteric work (often unbeknownst to those who employ them!) but not everything Dion worked with was unique to her. As can be seen from her useful modern biographies, especially "Dion Fortune and the Inner Light" and "Dion Fortune and the Threefold Way" (both by Gareth Knight, and based around "Society of the Inner Light" archive material), Dion was a high-grade trance medium, and her trance contacts provided her with much of her material. She also worked within a disciplined magical group, comprising a number of people with exceptional knowledge and talents.

She had some knowledge of the Glastonbury area from her childhood stay in Weston-super-Mare, but her first esoteric connection to Glaston seems to have been circa 1921, when she stayed at Alice Buckton's Chalice Well guesthouse and acted as a medium for Frederick Bligh Bond. Bligh Bond was embroiled in a complex web of spiritualism, archaeology and Rosicrucian Masonry at the time, and was receiving much material from an otherworldly grouping called either "The Watchers of Avalon" or "The Company of Avalon". The first seems to have been linked to ancient Hebrew or Phoenician mariners, while the second was a monkish convocation of spirits.

Frederick Bligh Bond's spirit informants had already provided him with much useful guidance during his excavations at Glastonbury Abbey ruins – a fact which seems to have contributed to his later dismissal from this project! – and they seemed happy to work with Dion Fortune as well. Bligh Bond's line of interest centred around the Joseph of Arimathea legend and the then-fashionable "British Israelite" interpretation of the origins of Druidry as an offshoot of Hebrew religion.

The contacts portrayed themselves accordingly. When working with Dion, whose interests were a balanced mix of Hermetic, esoteric Christian and "Nature Ray" elemental and faerie work, these contacts mutated into an array of characters more suitable for such work ... an interesting phenomenon in itself! Dion brought to Glaston influences from esoteric Masonry, Theosophy, two branches of the Hermetic Order of the Golden Dawn, esoteric Christianity, and the psychology and spiritualism of the day. The contacts obligingly interfaced with all this.

Bligh Bond brought architecture, spiritualism, Rosicrucian Masonry, a bit of Theosophy and quite a lot of the British Israelite world view, some of which he seems to have inherited from earlier (magical?) practitioners such as J.A. Goodchild, author of several works on the Hebrew origins of Druidry and early Celtic Christian culture and perpetrator of the intriguing "Blue Bowl" enactment (which truly deserves a separate long article to itself!).

Certain elements can be followed through the work of these predecessors, into Dion Fortune's realm and out of her work into the Glastonbury of the present day – it is illuminating to look at some of these and to follow their evolution insofar as we have yet been able to trace it.

First, let us look at the Round Table.

Arthur, in his mediaeval guise as the ideal king, has been associated with Glaston since around 1200 – linking Arthur's tomb to Glaston meant that Glaston must necessarily be Geoffrey of Monmouth's Avalon. Since then, Glaston has been a centre of all sorts of romantic and esoteric groups based on the Arthur/Grail mythos. The King Edward who created the Knights of the Garter was but the first of the monarchs who employed Arthurian lore to uphold their sovereignty. The Round Table at Winchester is another such tool, dating, in its present form, from Henry VIII's time – the same Henry who obliterated Glastonbury's Abbey in 1539.

Early on, the mythos identified the Round Table both with the table of Jesus's last supper and with the Zodiac – especially with the Zodiac used in Sufi and alchemical pursuits.

This esoteric side of Arthur's table was one of the things Goodchild sought with his "Blue Bowl" work. He wished to reactivate the table at Glastonbury/Avalon. Interesting, as it suggests that he knew – or thought he knew – of an early Round Table here which had been active in the past but had then declined.

The Blue Bowl was planted at a particular station on a pilgrimage route which may have had some connection with this earlier "table" – which in turn may have taken the form of a zodiacal array drawn out on the land (not to be confused with the later-discovered Katharine Maltwood zodiac, though the two may have causal links). All this occurred between 1898 and 1907 or thereabouts.

Around 1910, Wellesley Tudor Pole, one of the youngsters who found and worked with Goodchild's Blue Bowl, was given a series of rituals which supposedly related to a Tudor family order (called the Order of the Table Round) by a young man called Neville Meakin. Meakin was a colleague of Robert Felkin, head of one of the offshoots of the Golden Dawn, which later taught Dion Fortune. Both Meakin and Felkin were Freemasons. They were also part of a group of people allied to Rudolf Steiner, who were seeking to form an international Rosicrucian 'bund' (as in 'brotherhood'). We have copies of these rites, and they contain an esoteric version of King Arthur's Court, the idea of a zodiacal division of space, elaborate use of the same Glastonbury pilgrimage as an allegory concerning the elements, a developed use of knightly grades as levels of attainment, strong references to Lyonesse (the lost land beyond Cornwall) and a Lady of Lyonesse linked to Chalice Well. They also speak of a sevenfold spiral processional route up Glastonbury Tor.

It appears that the rites were rewritten by Meakin and Tudor Pole to incorporate the older pilgrimage – though the rites and pilgrimage might originally have been a unit, and simply revealed separately for some reason. The basic structure of the rites is identical to that of the outer Order of the Golden Dawn – the same version of the Tree of Life.

If all this had gone well, Glaston would have had its own pilgrimage and mystery rites combined. However, the death of Meakin from tuberculosis and the start of the 1914-1918 World War cut short that potential (although there is evidence that Alice Buckton used the pilgrimage, and possibly parts of the rites, in her work at Chalice Well during that war).

The Blue Bowl attempt showing every sign of having aborted, it seems that Goodchild passed on much of his knowledge to Bligh Bond in 1913.Perhaps Bligh Bond decided to try another route towards the reactivation of the Avalon Round Table, as his later work focusses on elaborate number symbolism and the zodiacal circle of huts in Joseph of Arimathea's old monastery at Glaston. This hut circle is directly comparable to the layout of the Winchester Round Table, and may well be intended to convey the same esoteric ideas.

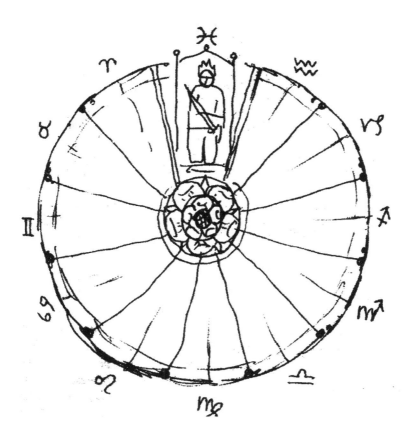

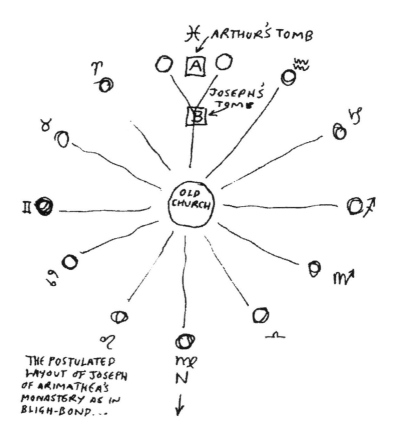

ARTHUR'S TOMB

JOSEPH'S TOMB

OLD CHURCH

THE POSTULATED
LAYOUT OF JOSEPH
OF ARIMATHEA'S
MONASTERY AS IN
BLIGH-BOND...

If this were the case, then Bligh Bond was out of luck. His occult work, a combative temperament and an acrimonious divorce combined to oust him from his archaeological work at the Abbey (and, indeed, from Britain). So it was left to Katharine Maltwood to step into the breach, which she did with flourish and style by creating/discovering her huge land zodiac whilst working on the illustrations for "The High History of the Holy Grail".

This wonderful construct is replete with ideas and images proper to the esoteric Masonry of its time (1929 onwards) and dovetails very interestingly with the earlier zodiac – which can be reconstructed from data in the pilgrimage and the "Order of the Table Round" rites. The Hood monument, and the Barton St. David church, are important in both zodiacs.

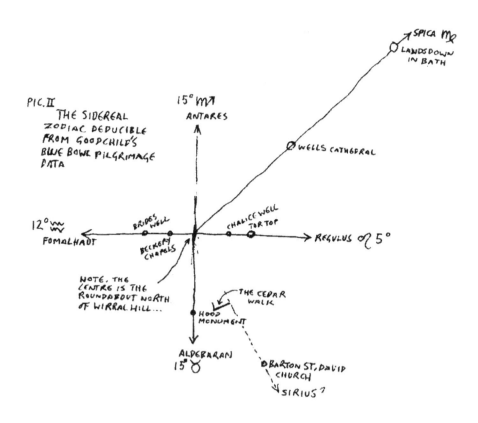

PIC. II
THE SIDEREAL ZODIAC DEDUCIBLE FROM GOODCHILE'S BLUE BOWL PILGRIMAGE DATA

SPICA ♍
LANDSDOWN IN BATH

15° ♏
ANTARES

WELLS CATHEDRAL

12° ♒
FOMALHAUT

BRIDES WELL

BECKERY CHAPELS

CHALICE WELL
TOR TOP

REGULUS ♌ 5°

NOTE, THE CENTRE IS THE ROUNDABOUT NORTH OF WIRRAL HILL...

THE CEDAR WALK

HOOD MONUMENT

ALDEBARAN
15° ♉

BARTON ST. DAVID CHURCH

SIRIUS ?

It is possible that Maltwood, too, became side-tracked by tantalising detail before her zodiac was fully operational, for Dion Fortune, circa 1940, was given (by her inner, and outer, contacts from Golden Dawn days) a complete system of Arthurian symbolism, the "Arthurian Formula", which formed the basis of her group's mystery work for some time afterwards. This system seems to have many components which were present in the old "Order of the Table Round" rites and Goodchild's work, but expressed, of course, in Dion's own idiom.

Since then, such folk as Aleister Crowley, Anthony Roberts, Robert Coon, Andrew Collins, and Paul Weston have all contributed further, either to the fine detail of the land zodiac or to the exploration of its workings and purpose. I suspect that the Round Table at Glaston continues to try to manifest to this very day.

Having sketched in our local Round Table, let's look at the "Heart Chakra of Britain" and the "Bride's Nunnery" aspects of the tradition. In Goodchild's Blue Bowl work, the work at Avalon/Glaston was a part of a much larger scheme. Put simply, Britain was the heart of a world-wide Empire, and Britain's spirit was becoming unhealthy and materialistic. If the soul of Britain could be renewed, its influence would flow out to uplift the whole Empire, so a magical "Triangle of Art" was set up to house the new spirit – if it could be called in. This triangle was actually a double one – three "brain centres" of Britain, and three "heart centres".

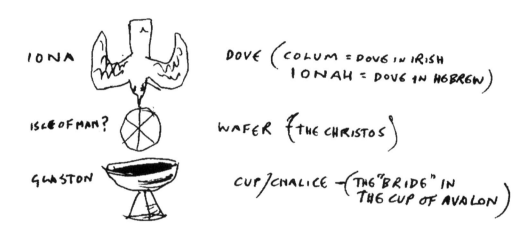

This was sensible, as Britain was seen as three countries with three capitals. The heart centres seem to have been chosen to make a neat triangle similar to that of the capitals, and because of links to the British Israelite myth of Queen Scota (or Tea Tephi) and her bringing of Jeremiah and the Stone of Bethel (later the Lia Fail and the Stone of Scone) from Israel. This is obviously another sovereignty myth – though why it was needful for Britain to have Hebrew sovereignty remains unclear.

Scota's tomb seems to be on Ireland's West coast, and the Stone of Scone was said to be Columba's seat on Iona.

This "net" of sites was connected to a complex set of ideas about uniting the feminine (Bride) nature of Avalon and the masculine energy of the "Isle of Sages" on Iona to engender a form of "Christos" presence which would renew these isles and reactivate centres of pilgrimage to transform the populace. The "Bride" spirit was a mixture of Mary Magdalene, Bridie of the Isles, the Qabalistic "Bride of the Microprosopus"(the lesser face of God), the Morrigan, and Goodchild's Tea Tephi. The "Sage" spirit seems mainly to have been Colum of Iona.

There appears to have been a sort of graphic pun here:

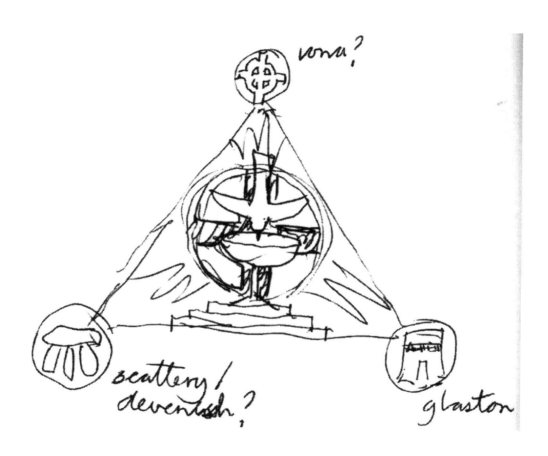

The heart centre of Ireland, by the way, seems to have been moved to Devenish Island sometime after the secession of Eire and before 1930, presumably to act as heart centre for Belfast, which was still a part of Britain. But that's OK, as St Molaise founded the Devenish monastery, and he was Columba's confessor.

By 1921, Dion Fortune had learned of the heart and brain centres from Bligh Bond's work (as Bligh Bond, in turn, may have learned them from Goodchild). Her book "Avalon of the Heart " seems to refer to the notion that Glaston is London's heart centre. Indeed, Dion had working sites in both Glastonbury and London for some time, the Glastonbury one including land opposite Chalice Well and the Victorian reservoir now called the White Spring. In the logo for Dion's "Society of the Inner Light" the same ideas are reflected:

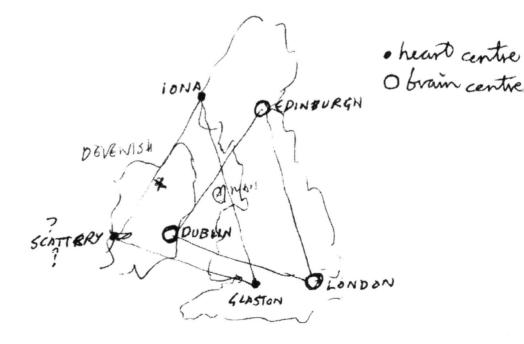

Presumably the corner sigils represent the Hermetic, Christian and Nature "Rays" of her work, but their orientations are interesting.

The London/Glaston corner bears the Hermetic sigil, which may hint at Dion's strong use of Isis imagery in the esoteric novels she wrote mostly in Glaston, and the Isis workings at the Belfry in London. [As an aside, Isis's glyph is blatantly present in Chalice Well as part of the well surround created by Alice Buckton and Frederick Bligh Bond in 1919; Isis in Glaston predates Dion Fortune and may derive from Golden Dawn sources or from Bligh Bond's Rosicrucian Masonic contacts.]

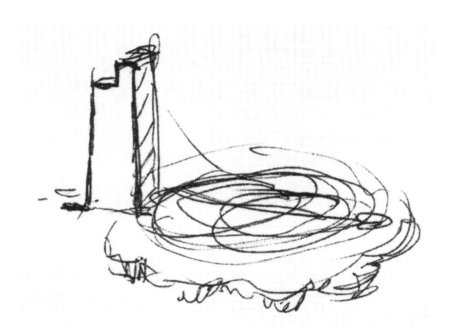

The idea of Glaston as a heart centre, either of Britain or of the world, seems to be a development of either late 1960s occultism or the 1970s influx of Eastern religions. It is a theme most elaborated in Robert Coon's work and later derivatives of this.

Bride's Nunnery now seems to be a pure Goodchild invention, as far as it is possible to track back at this point. William of Malmesbury, and his rewriter John of Glastonbury, claim that Bridget came to visit Glaston in the fifth century, and left some items which were stored as relics at Beckery chapel. No remains of buildings predating the eighth century have yet been found at Beckery, when a little wooden tomb-shrine (over a male burial) was surrounded by a cemetery.

There is a later story which has Arthur staying "at a nunnery on Wirral" and going down to the stone hermitage on Beckery to witness a curious Eucharistic miracle. This must date, at the earliest, to the twelfth century, when that stone hermitage was built. But Goodchild and his friends seem to have conflated it with the earlier story of Bridget's visit and the later attribution of the site as a Magdalene chapel (John of Glastonbury, probably late 1300s) – and woven it all into a story of Tea Tephi's enlightened Druidry being suppressed, going underground as the Bridget Cult, and having an outpost on the "great fish idol" at Beckery ridge at Glastonbury. (For the full story, see Patrick Benham's book "The Avalonians".)

Alice Buckton took up the theme in her play "The Coming of Bride" in 1914. It is a reworking of a Fiona MacLeod drama of the same name, but moves the ending to Glaston instead of Iona. The story also appears in her version of the Blue Bowl pilgrimage.

After her, the story seems to go into hibernation until its rediscovery at some time in the 1960s or 1970s, when it is worked into the local women's spirituality world view. Some time then, the old Beckery ridge end, where the chapels were, is renamed "Bride's Mound" and given a strong esoteric focus relating to both pre-Christian and Christian "Bride" ideas. Goodchild's esoteric fable, concocted perhaps to empower his Blue Bowl enactment, has become history and a truth no true believer would deny.

Another ingredient in the Blue Bowl pilgrimage has suffered a similar fate. In 1902 Wellesley Tudor Pole first walked the Glaston pilgrimage. This route included a seven-turn spiral to the top of Glastonbury Tor, which had to be reached at sunset so that the pilgrim could attune to the sun setting in the ocean in the West. This is a truly powerful experience even without the spiritual preparation such a rite would normally include. This rite, or it's like, may be very old indeed, and has a faint odour of the old native form of worship whose purpose was to open the golden road to the lands in the West. No more may be said of this, as these rites are experiential and words simply impede them. The Order of the Table Round rites place this climb in an Arthur/Archangel Michael context, and give a different form of preparation. All of this dates to about 1910-1911.

The spiral way up the Tor resurfaces in Dion Fortune's work with the elements, and in her book "Avalon of the Heart", but it then vanishes from sight again until the 1970s, when it reappears in the Geoffrey Russell article in "Glastonbury: A Study in Patterns", where it is described as a seven-turn Cretan labyrinth. This idea was opened further by Geoffrey Ashe in a small booklet on the subject, and has since been adopted as proven ancient history by many Pagans and Goddess worshippers – a fine example of the birthing of a modern legend.

Perhaps the most curious of the themes which moves into and beyond Dion Fortune's work is the idea of the "Hill of Vision". This concept seems to be genuinely old. It has resonances in the "Mound of Arberth" in the Mabinogion where Pwyll first encounters Rhiannon, in the white hill which stands to the South of the Otherworld crossroads in the lore of the Old Religion, and in the white hill which features in alchemical symbolism. All relate to the purification and empowerment of inner vision. It is notable that the Tor is a prominent hill set to the South of the holy island of Glaston – a perfect place to embody the White Hill of the South.

In Goodchild's work, the famous Blue Bowl comes from a recess in a wall of a ruined monastery in Albegna near Bordighera in Italy – a village whose name is built around the Latin "Alb" root for "white". The bowl is a tool of illumination, empowerment, and inner vision – a diary was kept of the visions seen in it.

Bligh Bond used the title "Hill of Vision" for one of his published collections of channelled scripts – all of them on the themes of prophecy and the state of Britain after the (then current) 1914-1918 World War. Such scripts were very much in the spirit of the time. Whether Bligh Bond equated the Hill of Vision with the Tor is unclear, but it is possible. The hill was attributed to Michael, the angel who guides and protects the souls of the newly dead – a logical empowerer

101

of visionary contacts with the same.

Dion used the "Hill of Vision" very much as the Tor, especially in her wartime workings when transformative visions were formulated in caverns within the Hill. This material has been occasionally reworked by the Society of the Inner Light and others up to the present time (see Paul Weston's restating of it in the late 1990s), and appears to be still quietly evolving in the Otherworlds.

Perhaps the strongest themes in the ancient Glastonbury tradition are these three:

> Rites of National Sovereignty,
> Rites of Entry to the Otherworlds, and
> Rites of Transformation or Initiation.

The strands discussed weave together to form a structure, always on the verge of entering physical manifestation, which can serve all three goals.

Deeper than all these, however, lies a function which serves the well-being of the planetary soul. Dion Fortune's Atlantean imagery of Sun/Mountain and Moon/Sea temples relates to this and provides a means by which humans may glimpse, and possibly serve, these vast concerns and age-long transformations.

And then, of course, there are the Dragons and their Queen. But that's another story...

*Avalon Magazine, Issue 28, Autumn/Winter 2004*

# NUMBERS AND THE ABBEY

**Alan Royce** *follows in the gematrial footsteps*
*of Frederick Bligh Bond and David Fideler.*

Ever noticed how things move in spirals? Back along I wrote an exploration of the number patterns on which the Mary Chapel was based, and showed a little of how these numbers were manipulated to form an actual building.

Since then I have had time to read more of Bligh Bond's work and to struggle with the ancient Harmonic Science expounded by David Fideler. This has led me to look again at some numerical and gematric themes underlying Bond's Glastonbury work. Interesting clues abound both in his writings and in his actual designs. Both are quite accessible for the standard fees...

One of the most accessible is the wrought iron design on the outer/top surface of the Chalice Well lid (not the inner one, which was created circa 2000 by Hamish Miller – fine work but at a different scale). Take a tape measure and look at it yourself, but be prepared to deal with awkward angles, distorted circles, strips of iron which can be measured to either side or to their midlines, etc. etc.

Don't worry overmuch about absolute precision. The Harmonic Science is about just that, the conscious harmonisation between the absolute perfection of the One and the fluid chaos of the Many – Apollo with his music representing that mediation tending towards unity, Dionysos with his revels representing that mediation tending towards the Many.

This two-faced divine process is modelled rather well in modern Chaos Theory, in which chaos is seen to be orderly, and order fundamentally chaotic.

But back to our ironwork. Here (*fig. I*) is the well in its setting, as created by Alice Buckton, Frederick Bligh Bond and numerous friends in 1919. The Star in the East and the variously-numbered 'stairways' in the directions seem to be Masonic references – not surprising, as Bond was a Freemason and had many Masonic friends - but the well design itself seems more specific to Glaston's own story, at least as Bond conceived it.

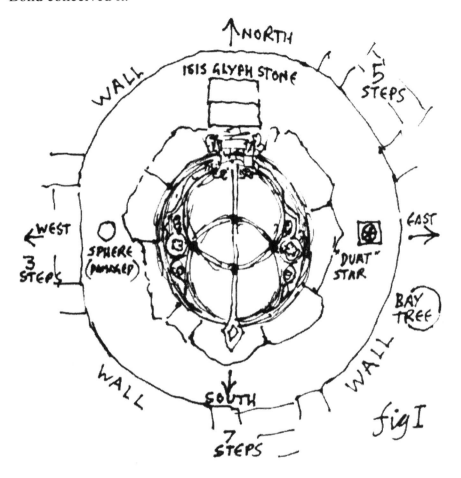

The stone in the North seems to be a version of the 'throne' hieroglyph borne on the head of the Goddess Aset (Isis in Greek). She could be read as the Stellar, Nocturnal and perhaps Underworld Mother of Horus, that bright power who arises in the East as dawning light. The foot of the stone bears the hinge, out of which the Vine arises, curving to either side of the central design, and bearing fruit to East and West. The Vine speaks of Dionysos, Jesus, Wine, Blood, and to the Davidic Bloodline so important in early Christian lore – see the Didaché.

David was a sort of Hebrew Apollo, calming souls with his lyre and psalms. Horus and Apollo were melded together in later Egyptian symbolism (under Greek rule) to imply that the East/West axis was the way of salvation. The Spear, also the 'hinge' of the design's symmetry, heads North to South, like the 'Cardo' of Etruscan/Roman Augury. Its blade is the means of opening the well, as a spear will open a wound. Lift it and note the 'meridian sun' on its lower surface.

Bond, in fact, sees this well as the Wound of Christ, opened by the spear of the blind legionary Longinus, which released Blood and Waters 'from the heart'. Longinus can represent the many (legion) in their lack of spiritual vision (blindness). His blindness is healed by the issues from the wound (he is initiated into the Light of understanding).

The 'Wound' is portrayed as the Vesica Piscis between the Northern circle of the Many and the Southern circle of Divine Unity. This Vesica has been used to indicate the Womb of the Virgin (with Christ in it, see later) or the Wound, as stated, or the Heart itself, as the mediatory organ of the body as microcosm ... the Heart as Leo in the Zodiacal Man. Is this one reason why the waters now issue from a lion's head in the heart of the garden?

One wonders whether Wellesley Tudor Pole consciously arranged his new acquisition in the form of the 'Three Worlds' of Greek spiritual anatomy: Head as Nous or Mind, Breast as Thymos or Soul, Belly as Epithusia or Appetites.

Wellhead, lion's head, and King Arthur's Court, perhaps (as the gardens ended there when WTP took them over in mid-January 1959 – just in time for Imbolc!).

Having sketched in Bond's view of the Well as the 'Grail' of Jesus' waters-and-blood, let's look at his numbers.

The middle Vesica is the key. Each axis has three measures (*fig. II*).

We need these measures in inches – Bond and his friends would have scorned centimetres in a sacred context – and we can then use the array of tools available to explore further.

Don't take the measures too seriously – the lid is by no means easy to measure accurately – but they will suffice, as you will see.

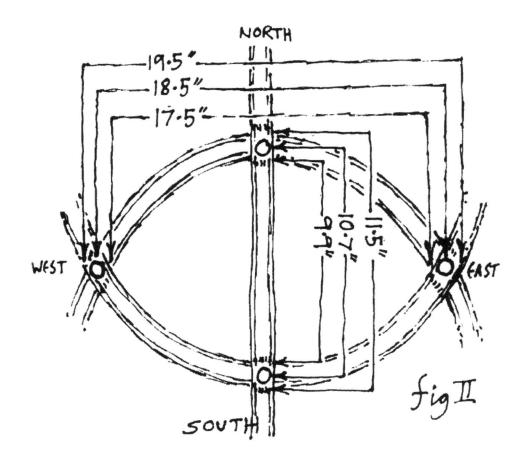

fig II

Given that the lid was fitted in 1919 (at Samhain), and designed earlier, we must do this properly and limit our comparisons to Bond's pre-1919 work. This still gives us his two works on gematria with the Reverend Simcox-Lea, and his book on the use of automatic writing to explore the architectural history of Glaston Abbey. All these books should be read carefully in the original before serious work on the Abbey archaeology of that time is attempted. Bond's actual position on many matters is sometimes surprisingly different from the way later commentators portray it.

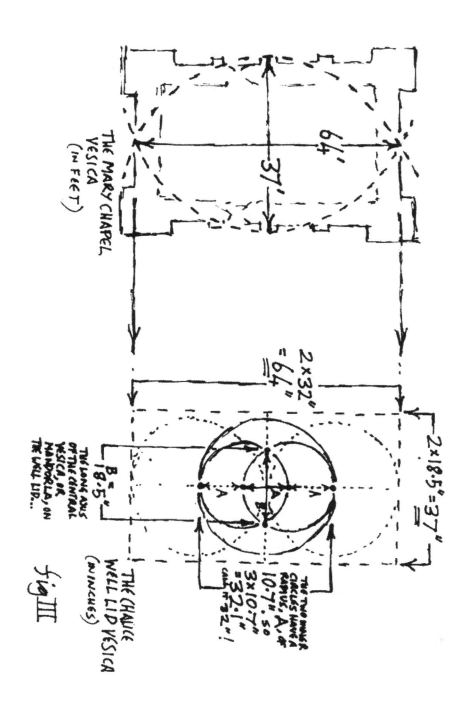

THE MARY CHAPEL VESICA (IN FEET)

64'

37'

2 × 32" = 64"

2 × 18·5" = 37"

B" 18·5"

THE LONG AXIS OF THE CENTRAL VESICA, OR MANDORLA, ON THE WELL LID...

THE CHALICE WELL LID VESICA (IN INCHES)

THE TWO INNER CIRCLES HAVE A RADIUS, A, 4"

10·7" SO 3×10·7" =32·1" (ALL FT. 32·0"!)

fig III

But back to our numbers. Bond speaks of numbers in two main ways in relation to the Abbey; the proportions of the Mary Chapel, and the length of the whole Abbey church. The first is part of the discussion on the Vesica proportion, its gematria and its links with different unit measures, while the second is very important to his argument that the great church was aligned upon a master grid of 74-foot squares.

Let's do the Mary Chapel first, as its connection with the Chalice Well lid design is clear and simple (*fig. III*).

There is no need to explain this really – change the units from inches to feet and you can map this expansion of the lid's central Vesica directly onto the Mary Chapel values.

Bond explains in his 'Apostolic Gnosis' that many Greek phrases linked to Jesus add up to multiples of thirty-seven. He specifically says that the area 37' x 64', or 2368 square feet, equals the total of 'Jesus Christ' (in the Greek alphabet) in gematria, and that half of this, the area of the two equilateral triangles in the Chapel Vesica, adds to 1184, the date of the Chapel's design (and of the fire which deleted the original?).

Bond points out that other Vesicas can be derived from the Chapel plan. He specifies three, including the previous example, but does not give measures for the other two (*fig. IV*).

My own work in this line (The Joseph Chapel, for an early attempt) approaches the problem via the Latin gematria in the IESVS-MARIA stone set in the South-facing outer wall of the Chapel. IESVS adds to 67, MARIA adds to 38, giving another Vesica which relates quite well to the building.

These numbers, when expanded and turned to inches, then feet, define important dimensions of the internal space (*fig. V*).

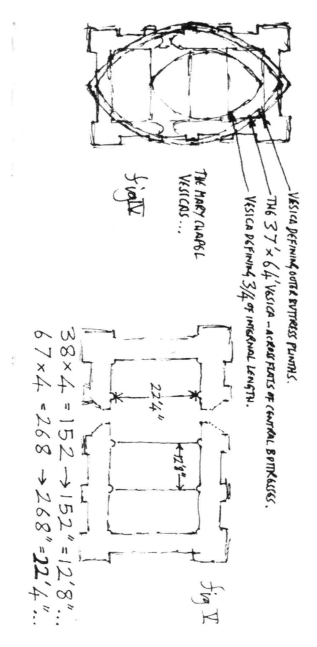

Fig.IV

THE MARY CHAPEL
VESICAS...

VESICA DEFINING OUTER BUTTRESS PLINTHS.

THE 37' x 64' VESICA — ACROSS FLATS OF CENTRAL BUTTRESSES.

VESICA DEFINING 3/4 OF INTERNAL LENGTH.

22'4"

12'8"

38 x 4 = 152 → 152" = 12'8"...
67 x 4 = 268 → 268" = 22'4"...

Fig.V

It is even possible to approximate Bond's own figures using the IES-
VS-MARIA figures, based on the grid of Vesicas which Bond overlay-
s on the Chapel in a late work ('The Mystery at Glaston', I think)
(*fig.VI*).

109

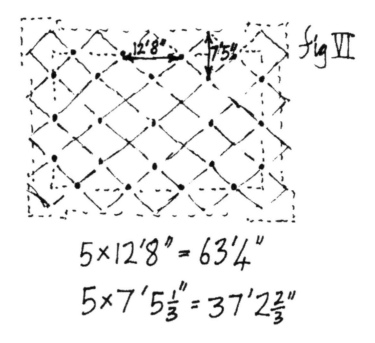

$$5 \times 12'8'' = 63'4''$$

$$5 \times 7'5\frac{1}{3}'' = 37'2\frac{2}{3}''$$

But this is cheating. Bond had not written this when the well lid was fitted. Now, can we divine our 38' x 67' from the central Vesica of the well lid? Try this, using the largest measures (*fig.VII*). Not so wonderful, really. But if you tweak the figures to 19" and 11.1" then the fit gets quite good: 38" x 66.6".

As I have seen no evidence that Bond ever used this Latin gematria, the above is something of an arithmetical entertainment, but the number 666 is quite relevant. To see why, we must look at Bond's other interest, the length of the Abbey. Here is Bond's plan, rather simplified (*fig. VIII*).

The perimeter of this grid is 5 x 74' (370') by 9 x 74' (666').

This is an interesting fusion of our 37 x 64 and 38 x 67 Vesicas, and in Bond's book the 5 and 9 are barely indicated. But the numbers here are so redolent of an ancient pattern related to the Sun – the visible face of the Gods at Mediation – that they must have been quite irresistible.

110

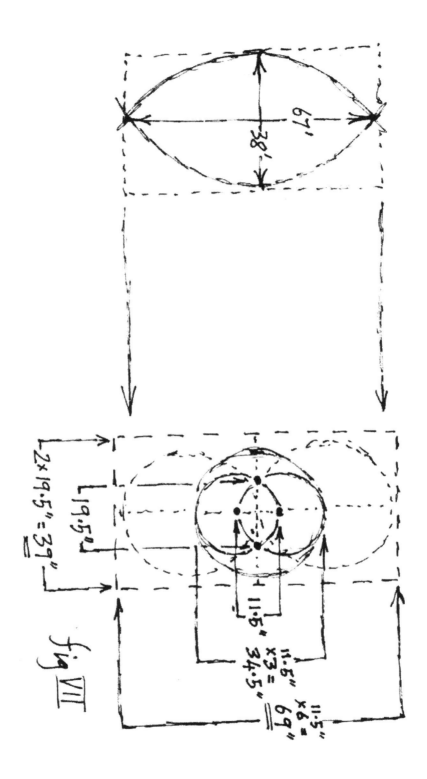

67'

38'

2×19.5" = 39"

19.5"

11.5"

11.5"
×3 =
34.5"

11.5"
×6 =
69"

*fig* VII

111

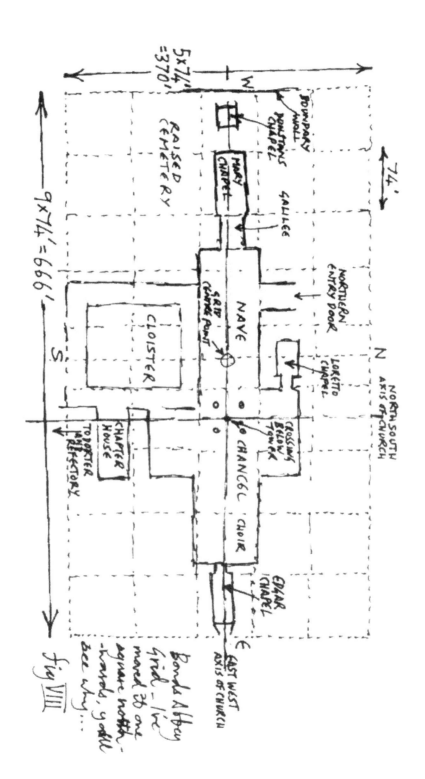

Fig VIII

112

Here is the pattern (*fig. IX*). It is called the Kamea, or magic square, of the Sun.

| 6 | 32 | 3 | 34 | 35 | 1 |
|---|----|---|----|----|---|
| 7 | 11 | 27 | 28 | 8 | 30 |
| 19 | 14 | 16 | 15 | 23 | 24 |
| 18 | 20 | 22 | 21 | 17 | 13 |
| 25 | 29 | 10 | 9 | 26 | 12 |
| 36 | 5 | 33 | 4 | 2 | 31 |

And here are its relevant properties:

      sum of any four symmetrical numbers = 74 (2 x 37).

      total along any line = 111 (3 x 37).

      sum of perimeter = 370 (10 x 37).

      sum of whole square = 666 (18 x 37).

The numbers 111 and 666 were considered, in Hebrew gematria, to be those of NAKIEL, the Intelligence of the Sun, and of SORATH, the Spirit of the Sun, respectively. This is the Sun seen as mediating and harmonising 'logos' between the Divine Unity and the changeable mortal world 'below the Sphere of the Moon'. It is also obliquely mentioned in the 'Apocalypse of John' in the bible, as '666, the number of a man' – presumably a man who embodied 'Unbalanced Solar Authority' in that context.

The number is considered by some scholars to point at the much-disliked emperor Nero, 'Nero Caesar' being 666 in Hebrew and 1332 (2 x 666) in Greek. The Hebrew spelling is questionable, but John wrote in Greek.

Our interest, and Bond's, however, is not in the demonic but in the positive aspect of these numbers and their links to Christ as the Spiritual Sun, Mediator between God and Humanity.

Here are our 'Jesus' numbers again:

| | | |
|---|---|---|
| 74 (the corners, or cornerstones?) | 2 x 37 |
| 111 (the lines) Intelligence of Sun | 3 x 37 |
| 370 (the walls) | 10 x 37 |
| 666 (the whole) Spirit of Sun | 18 x 37 |
| 888 'Jesus' in Greek | 24 x 37 |
| 1480 'Christ' in Greek | 40 x 37 |
| 2368 'Jesus Christ' in Greek | 64 x 37 |

(which is the Mary Chapel, as shown above)

Oh, and we also have:

1184, which may be more than a mere date   32 x 37

One thing Bond does point out is that 74 feet is 888 inches, whose meaning is given above.

What Bond doesn't tell us is that 74, in Latin gematria, is the total of AGNVS DEI, the 'Lamb of God'. This interplay of Latin and Greek gematria is evidenced in other aspects of the Abbey, but more of this later, as it follows from our next line of thought.

The IESVS MARIA stone shows IESVS above MARIA, almost as if the heavens are IESVS and the earth is MARIA. It might be more accurate to say that the Ideal or Spiritual is IESVS and the Bodily or Natural is MARIA. In humans the immortal NOUS and the changeable PSYCHE – in the Abbey the Church as the Body of Christ laid out upon the consecrated Land.

The notion of MARIA as land is shown nicely by the fact that the Latin gematria of the Abbot's land-book, the 'SECRETVM DOMINI' or 'Secret of the Lord' is 152, which is the number of MARIA in Greek gematria.

The 38 of Latin MARIA becomes the 152 of Greek MARIA if multiplied by 4, the number of the elements, directions, and the Greek letter delta, which symbolises the source and wellspring of life, the Delta of Venus, no less.

Another delightful example of this type of number riddle is the terra-cotta amulet found in one of Bond's digs, now in the Abbey museum (*fig. X*).

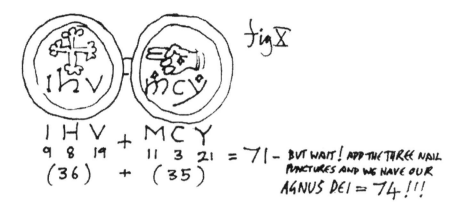

*fig X*

I H V + M C Y
9 8 19    11 3 21 = 71 – BUT WAIT! ADD THE THREE NAIL
(36)  +  (35)              PUNCTURES AND WE HAVE OUR
                                    AGNUS DEI = 74 !!!

Our 'AGNVS DEI' is a common image on Abbey properties. But we digress.

The Church as the Body of Christ on Mary the Land? 'The Fish in the Well of the Virgin' is an old description of Christ. We are thus led to the image of Christ in the Mandala, which is reminiscent of our look at Chalice Well. For the spear to wound Christ he must be where the Vesica is. This one is centred on his navel, which is Omphalos is Greek (*fig. XI*).

..CHRIST IN
THE MANDORLA
OR VESICA...

*fig. XI*

There is also an elegant little Greek graffiti design which tells more (*fig. XII*). This is another version of the previous image, but a little more abstract.

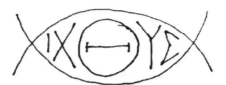

This is IXΘYΣ, the Fish in Greek, inside the Vesica Piscis, the "Vessel, or Bladder, of the Fish". Θ, or THETA, is the Omphalos of this Fish. It is also the Sun because of its form and a number *pun* :—

THETA $\Theta HTA = 318 = \Theta$

HELIOS $H\Lambda IO\Sigma = 318 = \odot$

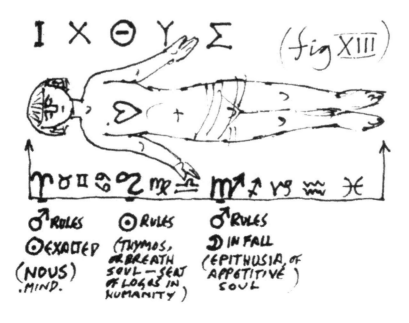

$I \quad X \quad \Theta \quad Y \quad \Sigma$ (fig XIII)

♂ RULES    ⊙ RULES    ♂ RULES
⊙ EXALTED   (THYMOS,    ☽ IN FALL
(NOUS)    OR BREATH   (EPITHUSIA, OF
.MIND.    SOUL—SEAT   APPETITIVE )
    OF LOGOS IN    SOUL
    HUMANITY )

The sun is at the central, mediating position of the old order of planets (Moon, Mercury, Venus, Sun, Mars, Jupiter, Saturn) and the body as Zodiac, wherein it represents the Heart, the seat of the Divine Spirit in humanity (*fig. XIII*).

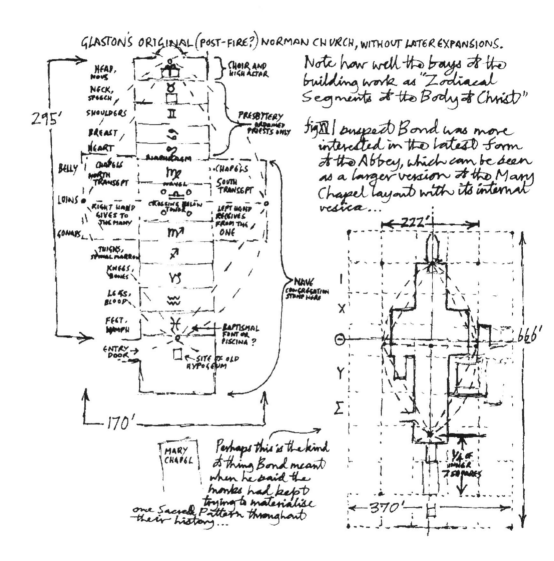

*fig.XIV*

It is said that many great cathedrals were modelled on the body of Christ in the Vesica. Is there evidence of this at Glaston? Given the difference in alignment between the early Mary Chapel and the later Norman Church (which is the one more likely to embody such thinking), let us try this (*fig. XIV*).

I think this should suffice. The old Abbey Precinct of Glaston has many hidden gems yet to be uncovered; depths whose exploration would be of spiritual value to both Christian and Pagan alike, as both spoke a common symbolic language in the first centuries C.E.

Frederick Bligh Bond saw the value in this, and others continue his work. Why not yourself? The Mysteries are not secret, they are open to anyone who cares to put in the effort of looking and listening, and unravelling the knots as they arise.

'To the sea, veiled ones' – 'to the presence of the boundless ocean of spiritual meanings, O Hidden Ones of God.'

*Avalon Magazine, Issue 41, Spring 2009*

# THE PITNEY PAVEMENT and the Glastonbury Zodiac

**Alan Royce** *interprets the mosaics of a local Roman Villa, and finds a surprising link to the Glastonbury Landscape Zodiac.*

In the early 1800s there were a number of gentleman archaeologists in Somerset whose hobby was the excavation and recording of Roman remains. Some of these gentlemen were more careful and thorough than others, and a number of their descriptions of these excavations survive.

The report which interests me, for reasons which may become apparent, is the record of a dig at a Roman villa site somewhat more North than West of the village of Pitney (West of Somerton). There is a summary of this report in the Victorian County History of Somerset (pp.326-328), which gives the general circumstances of the site, the form of the villa, and images of the mosaic pavements found in its South-West corner.

Below (*fig.1*) is a sketch of the mosaics in context, leaving out all colour and fine details in order that you will have a notion of what I am working on later.

What can we say about this set of mosaics? Well, first of all we can say that they form the floors of a ritual dining suite related to the Bacchic cult. The smaller room to the South is perhaps the dining space proper (with its three couches for diners to recline on, propped up by cushions and their left elbows), and the bigger space to the North the area for ceremonial, dance, etc. The odd little room with the boy striking at a serpent may have been for ritual ablutions, though there is no real way to tell nowadays.

# THE LAYOUT OF THE PAVEMENTS

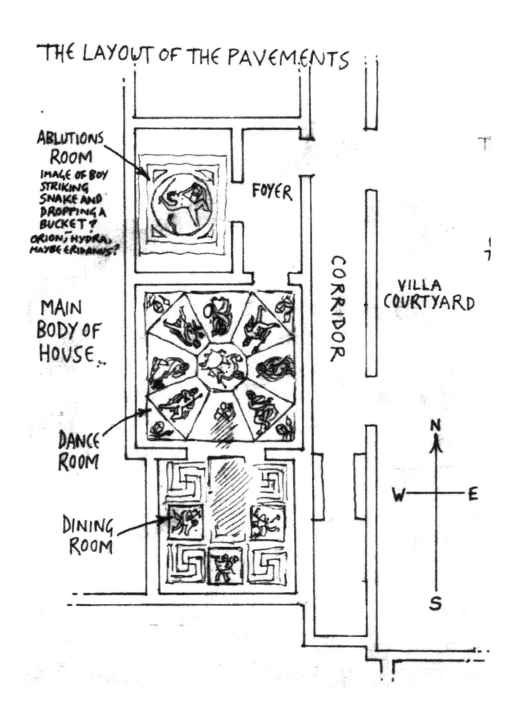

ABLUTIONS ROOM
IMAGE OF BOY STRIKING SNAKE AND DROPPING A BUCKET? ORION, HYDRA, MAYBE ERIDANUS?

FOYER

MAIN BODY OF HOUSE

DANCE ROOM

DINING ROOM

CORRIDOR

VILLA COURTYARD

N
W — E
S

THESE FIGURES SEEM TO BE SHOWN—

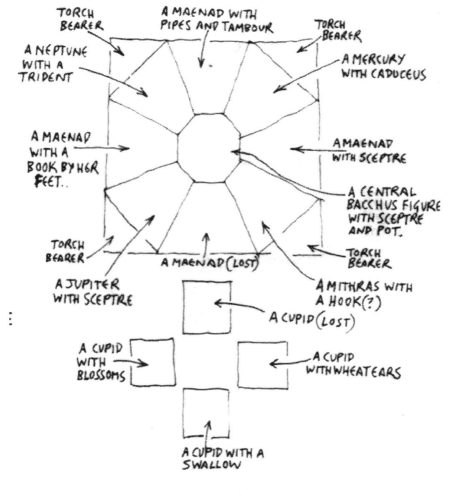

*fig. 1*

What can we say about the mosaics themselves? Well, this is where it gets interesting. Both large and small dining-space mosaics can be read as divisions of space, but in different ways. The eightfold structure of the large image suggests the eight winds. The God images on it suggest the rulers of the four elements, with the central Bacchus saviour-figure hinting at the line between the equinoxes. The smaller mosaic has (or had) four Cupids bearing the emblems of the seasons. Thus far we have the situation shown below (*fig.2*)

121

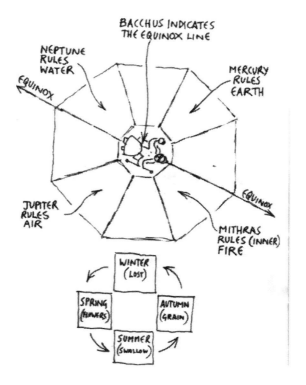

*fig.2*

The large room, then, has this as a zodiac. As you can see below, this is comparable to the layout in the little room.

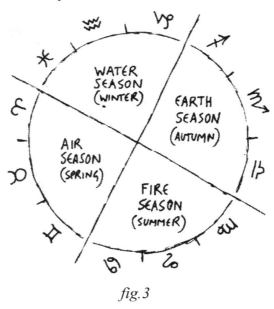

*fig.3*

We could leave it there, simply pointing out that a person entering by the offset doorway in fact looks in on a zodiac in the standard layout for the period.

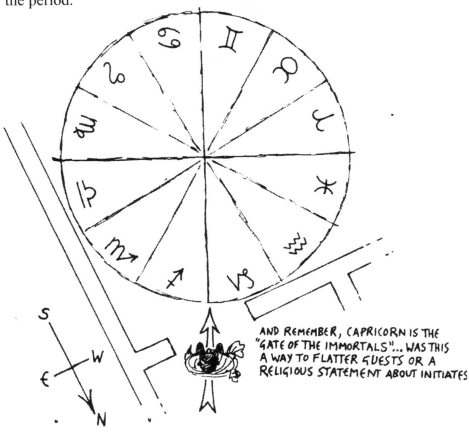

AND REMEMBER, CAPRICORN IS THE "GATE OF THE IMMORTALS"... WAS THIS A WAY TO FLATTER GUESTS OR A RELIGIOUS STATEMENT ABOUT INITIATES

*fig. 4*

However, where's the fun in that? There is another way to look at this dining space which is perhaps a little more surprising. In the related Cult of Mithras (he is in the mosaic, remember) the primary image in the ritual space is a tableau of Mithras stabbing the neck of a sacrificed bull to release the blood from its veins. This was a special moment in the process of a sacrifice, and was performed by a specific officer in the State Cult. Mithras is taking the role of this officer, but is liberating the sacred blood for the benefit of a dog and a snake, animals whose very presence would invalidate a sacrifice. Both animals represent po-wers of the Underworld. This 'gift to the Underworld' is obviously intended, as Mithras averts his face – a standard practice when offerings were made to such powers, but by making this offering Mithras is breaking a sacred law. The reasons for this apparent impropriety are not now understood, but must have been a part of the Mystery.

Our point here is that this tableau is about blood.

In some Mithraeums this tableau is mounted on a vertical axle, and can be rotated to show a different scene. This scene is of a meal at which Mithras and Helios are the guests at the top table. In many such images, a table bearing round loaves features. This side of the panel is about grain, not blood, though wine and grapes (symbols of blood in the related and contemporary Christian Mysteries) can also be present.

These panels vary considerably across the Empire, but in many the curious phenomenon of an overt and an implied zodiac can be observed (fig.5)

This is the 'bloodletting' zodiacal arrangement. So what happens when we flip the central panel to the 'dining room' scene? Voilà! (*fig.6*)

Now, doesn't that look familiar? This is exactly the layout of the zodiac in the larger room at Pitney villa, as seen by folk looking out at the smaller dining room. What would be seen on the end wall by ritual diners in a Mithraeum is seen on the dance floor by the ritual diners in a Bacchic space. At Pitney, however, only the inner zodiac is shown. The outer one is implied by details such as the Eastern Maenad's sceptre and the book by the feet of the Western Maenad (book = liber = Libra? Also, Liber is a Roman God equated with Bacchus and, sometimes, with Mithras).

Perhaps this kind of zodiacal display was used in many Roman Cult spaces. More work is obviously needed here.

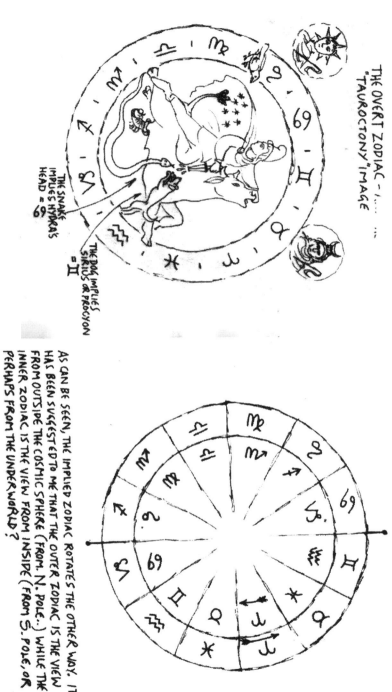

THE OVERT ZODIAC ~ ... ...
"TAUROCTONY" IMAGE

THE SNAKE
IMPLIES HYDRA'S
HEAD = 69

THE DOG IMPLIES
SIRIUS OR PROCYON
= Ⅱ

THE OVERT ZODIAC ...

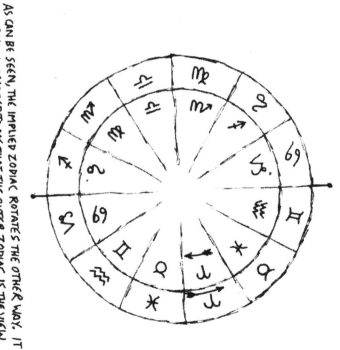

AS CAN BE SEEN, THE IMPLIED ZODIAC ROTATES THE OTHER WAY. IT
HAS BEEN SUGGESTED TO ME THAT THE OUTER ZODIAC IS THE VIEW
FROM OUTSIDE THE COSMIC SPHERE (FROM. N. POLE...) WHILE THE
INNER ZODIAC IS THE VIEW FROM INSIDE (FROM S. POLE, OR
PERHAPS FROM THE UNDERWORLD ?

*fig.5*

125

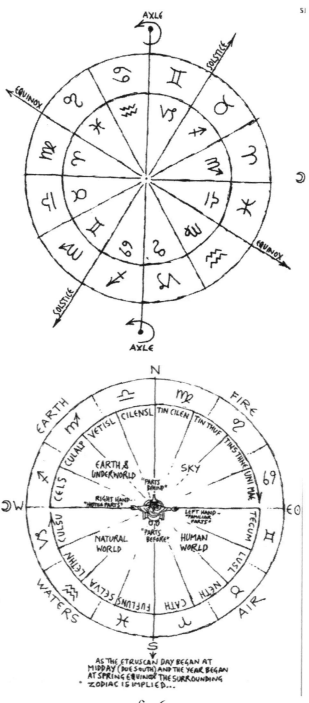

*fig.6*

However, we are not finished yet. One of the main reasons for a strong Roman presence in the Somerset area was the ample supply of lead (and the silver often found with it in the ores).

The real experts in metalworking in the Roman context were the Etruscans, who had been pretty much conquered and assimilated by Rome by the time that Britain was taken under Roman 'protection'. Bacchic cults were popular in Etruscan culture and were linked to metalworking. 'Fufluns' was the Etruscan name for Dionysos (Bacchus is a cult title for Dionysos) and Fufluns was the God of the Etruscan city called Populonia. Populonia was a major metalworking zone for centuries before the Roman takeover. Should we, then, expect an Etruscan reading of our mosaic floor? In fact, we can find one. Here is the division of space used by Etruscan Augurs when taking the omens for the inception of a new site or enterprise (*fig. 7*).

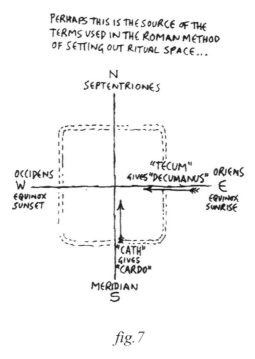

*fig. 7*

If we imagine the Bacchus in the centre of the mosaic to be an Augur on his seat facing a ritual (as opposed to an actual) South, the mosaic fits the above zodiacal scheme perfectly.

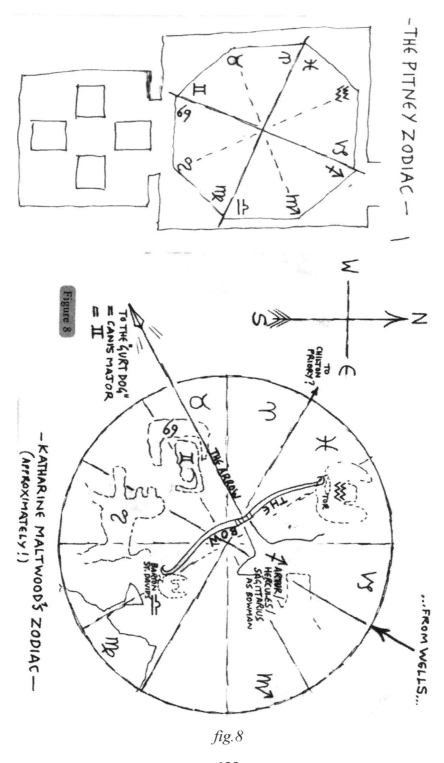

*fig.8*

By now, your head should be thoroughly turned around, so let's go back to the original, as portrayed in Colt-Hoare's delightful report, and look at a bit of more recent history. Another person of the early 1800s who took note of this report was William Stradling, a Bridgwater Mason who built a curious folly on the Polden Ridge called 'Chilton Priory'. He wrote an elaborate description of this somewhat esoteric edifice, and then moved on.

The structure passed through several hands and suffered somewhat, but was finally the country home of Katherine Maltwood and her husband. She certainly must have read Stradling's description, and she refers to the Pitney Villa mosaic in her 'Temple of the Stars' circa 1929. Perhaps, then, it is no surprise that her famous zodiac accords quite well with the more obscure one set up by a Bacchic initiate in the second century or so, close to an important military road and metal route near the Northern capital of the Romanised Durotriges (*fig.8*).

*Avalon Magazine, Issue 46, Autumn/Winter 2010*

# THE WATCHING OF THE ROSE

**Alan Royce** *gives us an overview of the mysteries and esoteric traditions of Glastonbury, and explains the significance of the Blue Bowl and the Rose.*

The very first article I wrote for Avalon, quite a few years ago now, was about the curious story of the Blue Bowl and its esoteric content. Though I have often looked at other things, this is a theme which refuses to go away.

This article aims to give a simple outline of our understanding of this local tradition of spiritual work as it stands at present. Perhaps the easiest way is to go through it in chronological order.

## 1898

John Arthur Goodchild places the Blue Bowl in an east-facing stone culvert in the raised bank of the River Brue near Beckery. This culvert becomes known as 'Bride's Well'.

Goodchild is a doctor and an antiquarian. His major influences seem to be British Israelite ideas and esoteric links to such folks as William Sharp/Fiona Macleod and the initiates of the Golden Dawn. The liturgy used in Bristol with the Blue Bowl contains extracts from Fiona Macleod's works and direct reference to the Golden Dawn.

The account, in a Psychic Research journal of the day, of the bowl's deposition speaks of a 'Ruby and a Gold Cross and Chain' being placed with the bowl (a reference to the 'Ruby Rose and the Cross of Gold', the Inner Order of the Golden Dawn, then run by W.B. Yeats).

The golden platter, said to have been bought with the bowl, is said to have been sent to 'the Sons of Garibaldi'. This could refer to Garibaldi's actual relatives, or it could be a reference to the Rite of Misraim, which Garibaldi headed for some time.

## 1904

Wellesley Tudor Pole takes the Triad of Maidens around the pilgrimage route in Glastonbury. This route is described, in the words of Katherine Tudor Pole, in Patrick Benham's 'The Avalonians'. The girls went round the route several times to open channels for spiritual power.

Also in 1904, Goodchild and Sharp met in Glaston, and the 'Triad Poem' was revealed. This poem was later expanded within the liturgy of the bowl in Bristol.

And yet further, in 1904, Rudolf Steiner purchased from Theodor Reuss the right to set up a lodge of the Rite of Misraim in Germany. He apparently did this to give a solid continuity between his own mystery teachings and the older mystery currents which he considered to be feebly embodied in the Misraim Rite. At some point after 1904 and before 1910, Robert Felkin and Neville Meakin – masons and members of a branch of the Golden Dawn – began to work in this mystery current with Steiner, Meakin being initiated into the German mystery.

## 1906
The Blue Bowl is discovered by the Triad of Maidens and goes to the Oratory in Bristol, where it is used as a part of a magico-spiritual endeavour to 'bring in light' from the higher realms. The bowl, the pilgrimage route, and so forth, are part of a system involving the reopening of the 'three heart centres of Britain' – Glaston/Avalon, Iona, and Eron.

This activity seems to have been partly to restart an Arthurian Round Table school in the Glaston area, and partly to employ a sort of sacred marriage between Brigit (as the Bride) and the Sages of Iona, to call in the new Christ impulse and renew the spirit of Britain. There seems to be a link here to the notion of a 'female second coming' referred to by Fiona Macleod in 'Iona' and to messianic ideas referred to more fully in Tau Malachi's 'St. Mary Magdalene'. The notion being that, until the feminine face of the Messiah is fittingly received, the masculine face cannot return...

## 1907 onwards
The bowl goes public, thus dispersing the power contained in the system of which it was a part. Glastonbury Abbey is bought by Jardine on behalf of the Anglican church. Frederick Bligh Bond, architect,

psychic researcher and mason, is employed to do archaeology in the abbey. He begins immediately to do psychic research into the abbey layout and history.

The Triad of Maidens slowly breaks up and is gone by 1910. Neville Meakin approaches Wellesley Tudor Pole to invite him into the 'Order of the Table Round', supposedly a Tudor family order. Wellesley Tudor Pole progresses through the grades of the order, but does not complete, as Meakin dies of consumption in 1912. The order is taken to New Zealand when Robert Felkin emigrates there in 1914.

The papers of this order describe rites which combine Arthurian chivalry, the Tree of Life layout peculiar to the Golden Dawn, and a version of the pilgrimage used with the Blue Bowl. The somewhat awkward interaction between the Golden Dawn base structure and that of the pilgrimage suggests to me that these were a forced marriage concocted by Wellesley Tudor Pole and Meakin – although the union might have occurred earlier, the two separate components of the same pattern being fed to Wellesley Tudor Pole by Goodchild and Meakin in turn. For our purpose, two diagrams are helpful.

1. The layout of the Lodge in the degree of 'Page' – the first level in the Order of the Table Round:

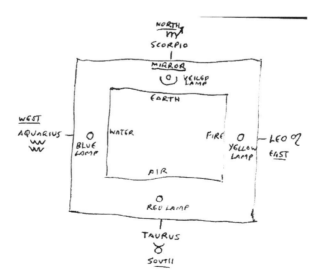

2. The layout of the pilgrimage, as described within the later 'Beau-mains' rites of the order, in which a young knight is tested by passage through the four elements. This was done in the lodge first, then enacted 'in real' by walking the Blue Bowl pilgrim route and performing suitable offerings and prayers on the way:

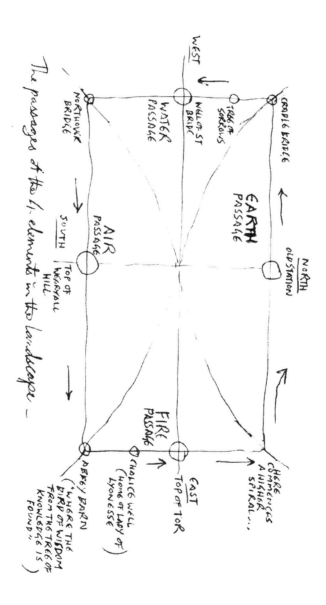

**1914 onwards**

Goodchild has died, the Great War has begun, Alice Buckton has bought Chalice Well and produced 'The Coming Of Bride' (a Glaston variant of a Fiona Macleod play of the same name). Frederick Bligh Bond has learned much gematria from Goodchild before his death – this begins to appear in Bond's later work.

There are records from 1915 and 1917-ish of the basic structure of the Order of the Table Round elemental passages being used by Wellesley Tudor Pole and Alice Buckton after Felkin's departure. These references are in a student's illustrated notebook (1915) and a book on Wellesley Tudor Pole's friend who was killed in France – 'A Pilgrim Soldier'. Both refer to the pilgrimage and to ceremony in the shrine at Chalice Well.

In 1919 a new well lid is donated to Chalice Well. This is an oak lid in a stone surround with an iron vesica piscis made by a London smith. It seems to be a gift of 'pilgrim friends', perhaps also from London. Bond writes of it a week later in the local paper and describes it as a depiction of the spear in the wound of Christ, the waters of the well depicting the 'blood and waters' from that wound. The whole thing is seen as 'a type of the Grail'. This probably ties in with Bond's interest in sacred measures and gematria in the abbey and the Joseph of Arimathea story. Joseph is said to have founded a 'Native British Church' long before the advent of Roman Christianity, which arrived in Britain with Augustine in the 600s.

This emphasis on the pre-Roman church is a feature of British Israelite thought derived from Protestant arguments put forward in the time of Elizabeth I and based on Glaston's earlier use of the idea that Joseph could have been its apostolic founder. This notion grew out of earlier Grail esotericism and followed naturally from the location of 'Avalon' at Glaston circa 1196, when 'Arthur's bones' were found there.

Bond later expended much effort trying to demonstrate the archaeological reality of Joseph's early monastery in the Abbey grounds (see *The Mystery Of Glaston*) and continued this interest after he was expelled by the Abbey trustees in 1922.

## 1922

Alice Buckton makes a film of Glaston's history. She also writes to an Irish friend describing the Glaston Bowl pilgrimage in detail:

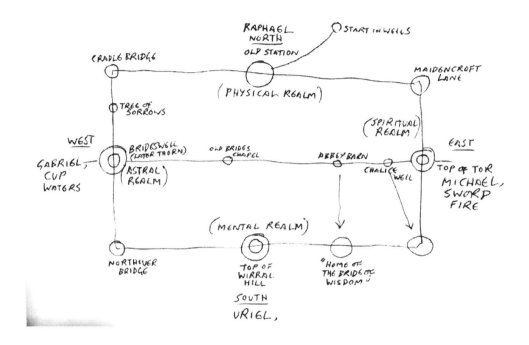

As can be seen, it is a variant of the 'Order of the Table Round' pilgrimage pattern. There is a new emphasis on the female mysteries and on the 'Watchers' of Avalon – an idea which has evolved out of the two directional watcher angels mentioned in the bowl liturgy. These 'Watchers' seem to be the Royal or Watcher Stars spoken of in the Book of Enoch and often equated with the four great Archangels:

| | |
|---|---|
| [Sun] | Michael |
| [Moon] | Gabriel |
| [Mercury] | Raphael |
| [Venus] | Auriel (or Uriel, or Phanvel) |

Interestingly, if we map these attributions onto the pilgrimage pattern in the 'Order of the Table Round' rite, we get the following:

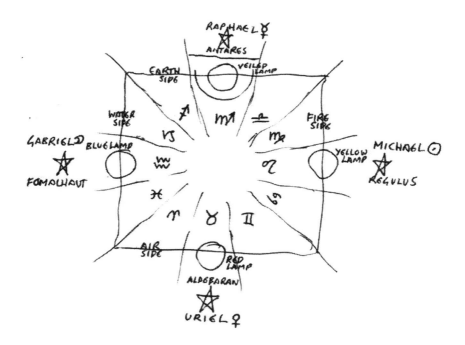

Now Aldebaran is a rose-red star in the centre of the sidereal Taurus, which is ruled by Venus. Regulus is a golden star at the heart of Leo, which is ruled by the Sun. The other two stars won't play this neat game, but consider this Tree of Life as described by Dion Fortune in her *Mystical Qabalah*:

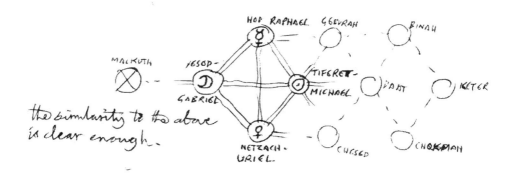

As for the elements in the directions – compare with the attributions used in Classical Astrology:

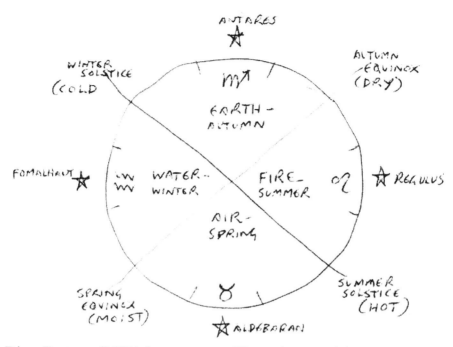

Dion Fortune (1921) has come to Glastonbury and has worked as a medium for Frederick Bligh Bond. In the coming years she will take up some of his work and expand it in her own directions.

## 1925 onwards

The Glastonbury Scripts are received by various mediums and collated. A common theme in several is the 'Rose Stone', a miraculous concretion of the blood and waters of Christ's wound brought to Glaston by Joseph of Arimathea. On their arrival on Wirral Hill they are said to have spent the night in vigil contemplating this stone. This rite is recommended for modern pilgrims too, but a red rose is to be substituted for the lost stone. The rite is a fast and vigil, contemplating the rose, over the night of 12th September each year. What is this about? Bond leaves us a clue:

This 'Rose Star' is found at the end of the rite's description. It is also found in his 1930s *Mystery of Glaston*, which deals at some depth with the ideas behind Joseph in Glaston.

The 'Rose Star', as previously hinted, is Aldebaran.

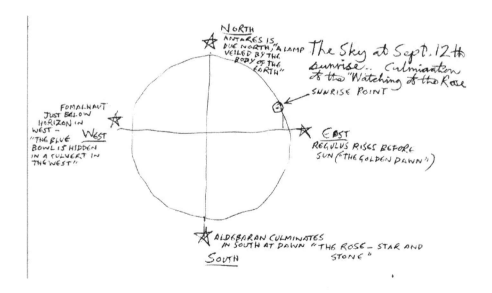

This suggests the alchemical red and white roses and their marriage:

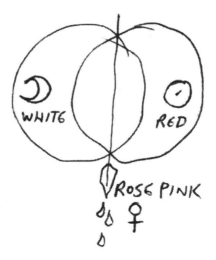

Any resemblance to the symbolism of the Chalice Well lid, I leave you to deduce for yourselves...

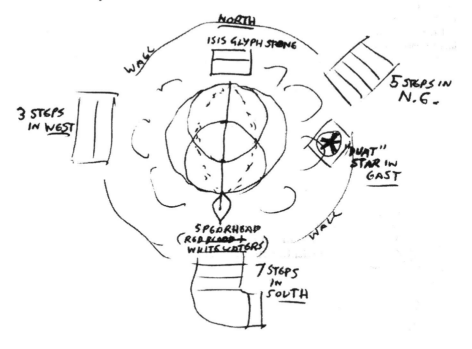

**1927**
Katherine Maltwood has discovered her own 'Round Table of Avalon'

which has only a couple of minor links to the zodiac implied in the Blue Bowl work. She is not impressed by the work of Glaston's occultists, as she states in her *Enchantments of Britain*. Bond has gone to America to work with psychics there, Dion Fortune is writing and teaching in London and Glaston, Alice Buckton maintains Chalice Well. By the 1940s all these presences have departed Glaston, and there is a quiet period.

## 1958

Wellesley Tudor Pole restarts the Chalice Well Trust begun by Alice. His old rival Ronald Heaver sets up a shrine in Keinton Mandeville, and is successfully kept out of Glaston by Wellesley Tudor Pole. This rivalry, according to Peter Caddy's autobiography, began circa 1925. It may have its basis in some sort of conflict between the British Israelite faction and those who followed Steiner's approach to the Mysteries. British Israel was strongly linked to British sovereignty and imperialism, and combined a strange quasi-historical ideology with undercurrents of genuine esotericism.

It is likely to have objected to Steiner's wish to balance Anglo American and Central European spiritual currents. Heaver and Wellesley Tudor Pole may well be examples of each current – Heaver having led British Israel for a time, and Wellesley Tudor Pole citing Steiner as one of his mentors.

Glastonbury seems to attract such conflicts. Even now all these currents are beginning to resurface – perhaps for another bout!

As George Santayana said, 'Those who do not learn from history are doomed to repeat it.'

*Avalon Magazine, Issue 37, Autumn/Winter 2007*

# THE THREE MOTHERS

**Alan Royce** *outlines his discoveries and insights about the ancient and symbolic European images called the "Three Mothers".*

A schist plaque from the Bath area shows a "primitive" (meaning stylised, symbolic, and perhaps native rather than Graeco-Roman in style) image of three female figures, side-by-side and facing the viewer. This old and simple version of the "Three Mothers", the Matres or Deae Matronae, perhaps gives a clue to the deeper intent of these common deities, found all over the Roman Empire.

They may be primitive indeed by Roman standards, but observe:

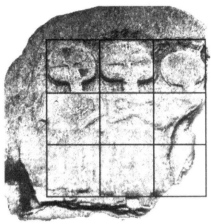

*The original image*

*The design is based around a nine-square grid*

Now, Peter Berrisford Ellis, in articles for the Irish magazine Réalta, argues convincingly that early Celtic astrology and Vedic astrology have common roots. So we note that this nine-fold grid, in Vedic lore, is often a grid of the planets. The Vedic system has nine planets, two of which are the nodes of the Moon, and are named after the sundered head and tail of a demon; Rahu and Ketu.

Venus, Sun, Moon, Mars,     Jupiter, Saturn, Mercury

Ketu  ♀  ☉  ☽  ♂  Rahu  ♃  ♄  ☿

In the Western (Greek/Chaldean) version of astrology, the planets are given in a different order, based on their apparent speed of motion against the fixed stars:

Moon (fastest), Mercury  Venus, Sun, Mars, Jupiter, Saturn (slowest)  then Ketu & Rahu follow after.

☽     ☿   ♀   ☉  ♂    ♃   ♄
1     2   3   4  5    6   7

Interestingly, we can reconcile these two systems using the Magical Square, or Kamea, of Saturn: the Square itself (note that all ranks and files add to 15) and the Square with planets.

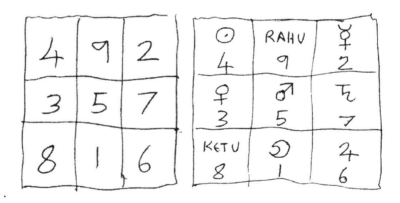

You will notice that mapping the Chaldean order of the planets onto the Saturn Square by number allows you to read off the Vedic order of planets.

143

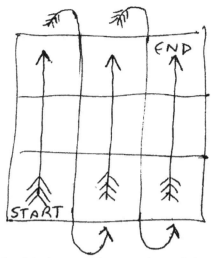

If this reading method is imposed upon the original stone image, we find ourselves with a sort of map of the order of planets broken into three "anthropomorphic personifications".

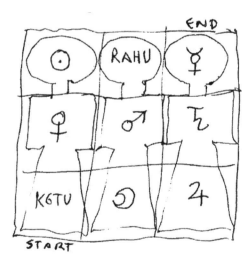

The Mothers as Kamea of Saturn and key to the planets.

Now this is all very interesting, but where does the idea of "motherhood" enter the picture? Patience, dear reader, while we add another thread!

144

Consider the idea of Siva-Shakti... the timeless Being/Potential of Siva is made actual by the power of Shakti. This expression of the totality of possibilities is achieved by the differentiation of Shakti into Qualities and Sequence.

The first division is into three Gunas, the "three mothers" of all expression and motion:

Rajas – energy, action, motion, beginning – RED.
Tamas – inertia, inaction, stillness, continuance – BLACK.
Sattva – brilliance, liberation, ending, illumination – WHITE.

This can be applied to our three "Deae Matronae" as three abstract mothers of all phenomena.

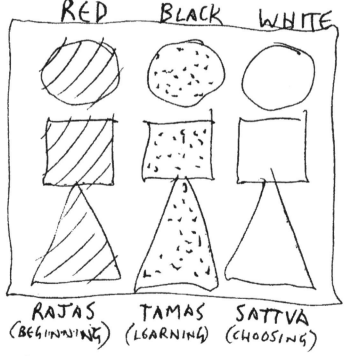

But we need not stop here. If we relate the simple hip/legs, torso and head shapes to their appropriate we can take the next step of permutation.

145

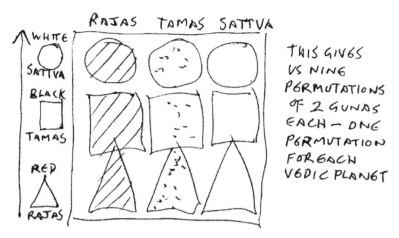

The nine planets as Guna permutations; 3 x 3 = 9

The next step of permutations gives us the twenty-seven lunar mansions of Vedic astrology – these are star groups notionally representing "days of the moon" but actually 13° 20' chunks of the ecliptic. Their correspondence with Sidereal zodiac signs is shown below.

| PLANET | GUNA COMBINATION |
|---|---|
| ☿ | ◯ + ◯ , SATTVA - SATTVA |
| ♄ | ◯ + ▢ , SATTVA - TAMAS |
| ♃ | ◯ + △ , SATTVA - RAJAS |
| RAHU | ⊙ + ◯ , TAMAS - SATTVA |
| ♂ | ⊡ + ▢ , TAMAS - TAMAS |
| ☽ | ⊡ + △ , TAMAS - RAJAS |
| ☉ | ⊘ + ◯ , RAJAS - SATTVA |
| ♀ | ⊘ + ▢ , RAJAS - TAMAS |
| KETU | ⊘ + △ , RAJAS - RAJAS |

The 27 Lunar Mansions as Guna permutations: 3 x 3 x 3 = 27

146

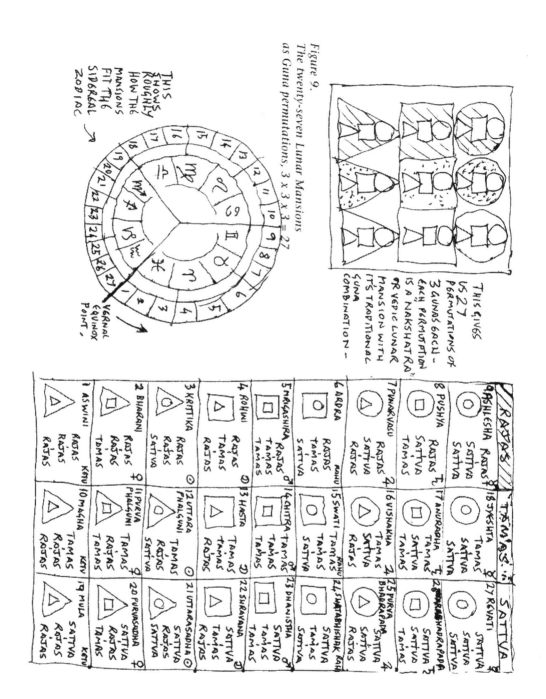

Figure 9.
The twenty-seven Lunar Mansions as Guna permutations, 3 x 3 x 3 = 27

147

If we were to take the next step in permutation, we would have the 3 x 3x3x3 = 81 array, which gives us the 9 x 9 board of the "Game of Sovereignty", but that takes us too far off our topic, perhaps.

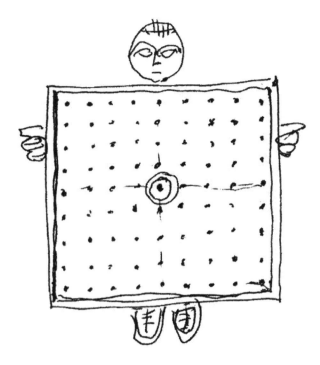

The Brandubh Board – an expansion of the torso of the 'Tamas' Mother as the Land?

This pattern can represent the twenty-seven days of the Moon's sidereal month (not its 29/30 day phase month) or the whole path of the Sun around the ecliptic. Both patterns naturally divide into thirds, and there are hints of nine-day "weeks" in old Celtic lore, and definite records of three-season years in both Greek and Egyptian antiquity.

Are there perhaps Goddesses of these ancient cultures whose natures support our extended speculation? Three main candidates come immediately to mind.

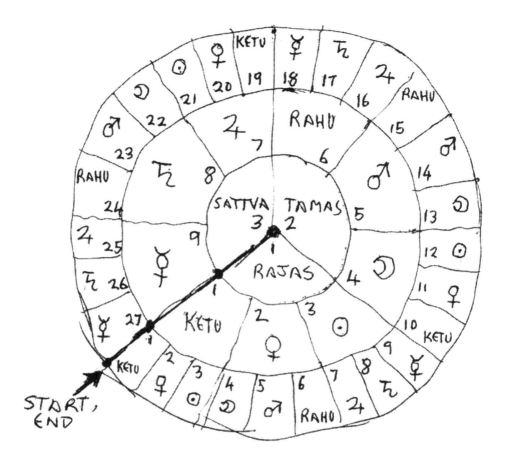

First, Hekate, mistress of all liminal states and places, one of whose common forms was a triple image placed at Trivia (crossroads where three roads meet). In later versions, each road was faced by a maiden with a different head (for example, Serpent/Hound/Mare, or Serpent/Hound/Lioness, or Bull/Hound/Lioness). These "three roads" could be literal roadways, or more abstract "roads" between three seasons, or where horizon, ecliptic and Milky way met, or even the ways connecting levels of reality. Hekate was not a simple Goddess...!

Second, the triad of Demeter, Persephone and Hekate, who formed the skeleton of the Eleusinian Mysteries. Their tale of the cyclic loss and reunion of mother and daughter with Hekate's help, seems to derive

149

from a mythic speculation on the yearly cycle of wild grain, another version of the three-season year (maybe a local adaptation of the Egyptian cycle of 'Flood', 'Sprouting', and 'Harvest'). As well as the seasons of 'Gestation Below', 'Sprouting' and 'Harvest', the three worlds are implied – Demeter for Above, Persephone for Below, and Hekate in her cave for Between. This Demeter-Persephone-Hekate triad is only the best known of a whole family of similar local Goddess triads. Karl Kerenyi analyses these variants most interestingly, suggesting they are but the various facets of one Goddess separated in cyclic time and endlessly being resolved. It may be useful to know here that 'Hekate' is a title of Artemis, as 'Hekatos' is a title of her twin brother Apollo – both words link to a term for "hundred" and another for "farshooting". Artemis, as the "bears who dance about the Pole", could be seen as the centre and source of all this cycling.

Our third example is perhaps an earlier version of this pattern – the Gorgon Medusa. She is a Libyan maiden rendered fearsome and mortal by Athena after mating with Poseidon in one of the former's temples. This Goddess liberates three powers from her blood as Perseus decapitates her – the winged horse Pegasus, the golden warrior Chrysaor, and many serpents. Signifying Sky, Land, and Underworld, perhaps? Asclepios, whose rod wound with a single serpent gives further hints, used blood from one side of her body to heal, blood from the other to kill. But – the Gorgon as a Goddess of seasons? Consider the ancient symbol of Sicily – the Gorgon's head at the centre of three running legs. Each leg was considered to be both a corner of the island, and one of the three seasons. The fronds between them were once, apparently, leaves, grain, and vine fruits. This ancient triskele was taken by the Normans from Sicily to the Isle of Man, for they ruled both places. And is not Man the centre of a triangular group of islands?

A systematisation of the early Greek Goddesses, reminiscent of my earlier Guna permutations, is unfolded by Adam McLean in his "The Triple Goddess". His system is most simply rendered as a circular diagram, whose form may by now be familiar. The subtleties should be gleaned from the author's text, rather than from my diagram!

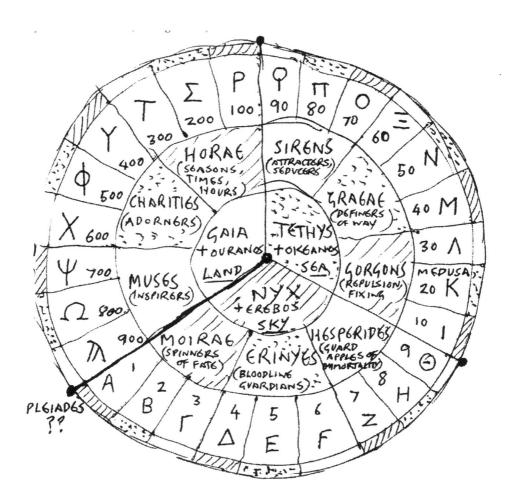

NYX (= Rajas?) = Unconscious.

TETHYS (= Tamas?) = Transitional states.

GAIA (= Sattva?) = Consciousness.

The notions of Beginning, Learning and Choosing are relevant here.

The three basic "Mothers" of Greek myth are in the centre, their daughter triads further out – I have added the Greek alphabet and its numbers for interest. You might also notice the Guna colours.

An interesting recent variant on the theme is the reference in Geoffrey of Monmouth to "the Goddess Morgen and her eight, or nine, sisters", who take Arthur for healing on their "Insula Pomorum" or "Insula Avallonis" in the West. Morgen, meaning "sea-born" suggests either Aphrodite or a daughter of Tethys. The sisters as daughters of Tethys, and thus as powers of transition between hidden and visible, conscious and unconscious, dead and living, would make good sense in this context.

Let whoever wills carry all this further, with my blessing!

*Avalon Magazine Issue 31, Autumn / Winter 2005*

# SALMON'S LEAP

*The ancient Druids welcomed Christianity into
Britain. Is the salmon carved inside the abbey
an acknowledgement of this?*

.... This article will be a playful, serpentine affair. There will be gue-
ssing. There will be artistic license. There will be make-believe. I am
going to imagine how it was to be here in the world-view of Roman
occupied Britannia, when the curious eastern cult of Yeshua the
Saviour from the Roman Protectorate of Judea arrived on these shores.

What happened here when the ancient Salmon of Wisdom leapt into
the new reality of the Great Fish, the ICHTHOS of the Middle East?
We can start with the Salmon. To know where to find the Salmon is
important. Salmon is present within much of what is now called
'Celtic' lore, but is most at home in the West, the place of harvest and
knowledge. John Arthur Goodchild was aware of this when he referred
to "the Salmon's Back" at Beckery; to the "Well of wisdom" at its
head. He was well versed in Celtic myth and in Christian sources and
was making a point in a magical manner.

In Irish lore, the Salmon floats in Connla's well, eating the fruits of
nine sacred hazel trees as they fall into the pool and incorporating the
wisdom kernels in the nuts into its very flesh. Each nut eaten formed a
purple spot on the Salmon's flank. Finn MacCumhall, leader of the
Red Branch band of warriors, attained his famed wisdom when this
salmon was roasted by him at the command of Fintan the druid, who
sought the wisdom of its flesh for himself. Finn's thumb was burned
when three hot drops of the salmon's essence spat out at him at the
point of its perfect roasting and he sucked his thumb to cool it.
Instantly, he imbibed the essence of the salmon's wisdom flesh,
becoming what Fintan had sought for much of his life to become.

It is interesting that our own Brythonic Finn, Gwynn ap Nudd, has a
palace beneath the Tor, a hill clearly visible on an interesting alignment with Beckery (or Bride's) Mound when viewed from Bride's
Well. Perhaps Goodchild intended this link to be seen suddenly as part

of a ceremony at that well. An initiatory technique, much as the curious tale about Finn imbibing wisdom seems to be a veiled reference to some initiatory technique of the old Bardic schools. This method of absorbing wisdom by touch is the proper means when in a state of Vision or in contact with Otherworld. Beings. A "higher octave" of touch is vastly important in such work.

In Brythonic lore, the well-known story of Ceridwen's Cauldron and the accidental enlightenment of Gwion Bach carries a similar theme. The newly-wise Gwion is chased, swallowed, reborn in beauty, bagged, tossed into the sea, and finally caught in Gwyddno Garanhir's Salmon Weir for the unfortunate Elphin to find. The supreme bard is become the Salmon, caught in the traps we set to try to frame wisdom. Elphin the Luckless becomes host to the greatest wisdom teacher of his age: Taliesin the "Radiant Brow".

In fact, Taliesin seems to have been a real person, Primary Bard of Urien of Rheged before that one lost his life protecting his realm from the Saxon mercenaries who had rebelled in the South East and were threatening to engulf all of Britain. Taliesin would have been a Bard who could combine the Bardic initiatory wisdom with the new vision of the White Christ, king of the Elements, revealer of new dimensions of Cosmos and Humanity.

Bards were a facet of Druidkind, the "People of Art". They specialised in wisdom. It would be their work to learn, assimilate and wisely promote to the other orders of society any useful, new ideas that came along. Christian ideas would have been processed by their colleges and would have been seen to be a fine and welcome expansion of an ancient and refined cosmology. Now, what was that cosmology and how did the Christ remake it?

First of all there was the Land, which was both the physical land which people came out of and went back into, and also the spiritual reality that the physical land was an expression of. The "ground" from which these two related expression arose was called "The Goddess". Her many forms reflected the different ways in which She was perceived to act and the different ways in which Her "children" could relate to

Her. The Goddess was the Whole and thus unknowable to Her children, who were by definition only parts of that whole. The fact that all emanations of the whole partake of the whole's qualities allowed them to know their Mother by analogy. This was Her greatest expression of love for them, which at the same time was an expression of Divine Self-Love. The faculty of awareness and will was called "The God". Many forms were envisaged to describe different modes and contexts of the operation of directed awareness. This was seen as the force for change and cyclic motion within the endless ground (or waters) of the Goddess. It manifested in individual person, in the relation of the Tribe to the land, which uttered it forth, and in the great transhuman processes of the world as a whole.

Each was a mirror of the other and all formed a living spiritual unity. In the cosmos, the pattern showed forth as a polarity between light and dark, fire and water, conscious awareness and unconscious sources, Summer and Winter, God and Goddess. Both "powers" were venerated; each was an essential part of the world process, meaningless without the other. The Dark came first and was the source of all, yet without the Light it could not change or be known. The Year was seen as a reflection of this spiritual process in cycles of time; the timeless or eternal reality mapped out in a form which supported and instructed aware beings (such as humans …). This process was stored in collective human memory as story and song – as myths of the Gods, Heroes, Demons, Goddesses, Kings, Queens etc. Different narrative forms grew for different audiences, for different purposes and social caste handled all such work. The Schools of Song, the Bards and Vates and Druids were respectively the collective memory, the means of mediating new patterns from the Underworld (the Goddess as dark source of all within person and earth) and those who wisely dispensed such knowledge to order society and its all-important relationship with the Land.

At the centre of this turning wheel of the cosmos was the World Tree, the place where the worlds of above and below met this world. Consequently, most work of spiritual meditation was described by analogies relating to trees, wood, woodwork etc. "Druids" can be read as "priests of the Oak". Science was referred to by the old Celtic terms for "wood". Divination was "the wisdom of the small sprigs" – often of apple! Bards were "carpenters of song". Song was the verbal expression of the upwelling of underworldly inspiration, the meeting of the stars and the deep earth in the spirit of the singer as a "child of Light", a unique, divine outpouring allowed by proper intent and awareness.

The illustration below (*fig.1*) is the Wheel of the Year as it relates to the world as a Whole. You will note that this is not the pattern used much in modern magic.

Neo-Pagan "Celtic" cosmologies are often derived from Kabbalistic sources with "Celtic Godforms" grafted onto that particular set of energy patterns. It works, it is internally consistent, but it is not Celtic and it is not linked to the Celtic overlay within the Land ... (a possible exception is Goodchild's curious work with the Michael / Bride polarity running East – West across Glastonbury. This intriguing structure amply repays investigation and may well have served to link up the otherwise disparate ideologies and magical systems ...).

The importance of Bride and Michael brings us to the more human layer of the old Celtic pattern. The survival of people depended on solidarity and intelligence. In other words, it depended on directed awareness harnessed to the goal of the collective. Indo-European cultures in general split this awareness into Functions. Three were aimed at the yearly struggle with the underworld forces, who would provide all if you had the courage and knowledge to pass their tests; the Fourth was aimed at maintaining the flow of contact between the worlds.

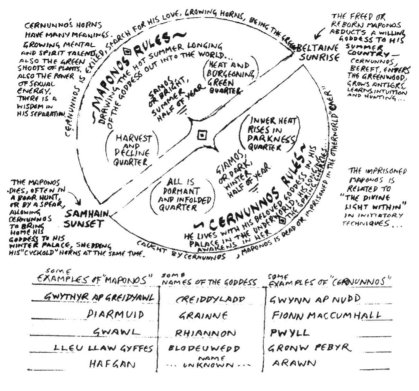

*fig.1*

The illustration below (*fig.2*) shows their general pattern. As can be seen from this image, Bride (as the "Water of Death" transformed by "Sunlight" into the "Water of Life") is the Muse of the 3rd function, whose work is the bodily maintenance of the people. Lugh (or in later times Michael!) watched over the high places, the upper reaches of human collective achievement, skill and awareness. He is a kind of reflection of Maponos in the human collective. The perfection of knowing, enabling the harvest of wisdom.

fig.2

In Glastonbury, these two muses have swapped places. Perhaps this is a device whereby the outer expression of one may be used to induce its opposite within the heart of a person working on that side (i.e. working with Bride at Beckery would induce "Lugh / Michael" qualities of skill and awareness in a person). In reference to this, note the images of Michael and Bride on the tower atop the Tor. Bride is above the outgoing door (she is "outside" in the landscape. Michael is above the "ingoing" door (he is "within").

This reflects well the idea just elaborated: Michael is the inner quality invoked by being in Bride's landscape and that inner quality is the one the Church wished to empathise with its bias towards Spirit.

This (*fig. 3*) seems to be the pattern that fits Glastonbury's landscape. It fits rather well and is well worth feeling your way into and getting to know, but we have neglected one position which is of crucial importance for the change from Celtic to Christian: the role of the King.

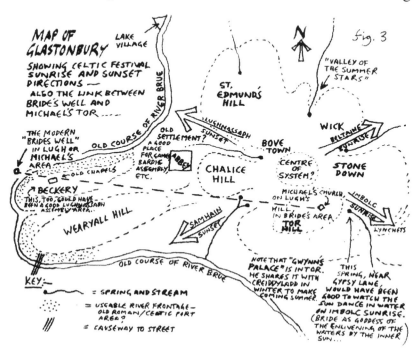

The King was the aware face of the cosmos symbolised in one person. He was the human version of the World Tree, the coming together of the Worlds. He was the one point where land and tribe formally met. This was symbolised in the ritual marriage he made with a representative of the Land in the form of the "Goddess of Sovereignty". In practice, this presence could be carried in the female royal bloodline, represented by one of a special college of priestesses, or even by the sacred animal of the "Sovereignty" face of the Goddess, such as the sacred White Mare … To make the pattern more authentic, there were often ritual acts to attune the king to relevant parts of the year stories. In some cases, he was "lopped" like the tree he was and put back in the earth at the proper time. This kind of understanding of Kingship allowed the collective Bardic memory-line of Celtic culture to readily understand the way in which Yeshua of Judea revealed his message to the world. His images of fishes and grain made perfect sense to them. Yes, the salmon was the direction of effort to the very source of wisdom, leaping up against the downflowing "waters" of stellar qualities till the very source was reached. Yes, the salmon's flesh was pure, distilled wisdom and to partake of his flesh was to become him, in the vision of the scholars of Bardic initiation, and did not Yeshua offer his "flesh", that is his wisdom and his spiritual nature, as a gift to all? These things were easy to understand for people who knew the sacrifice their kings had once made and understood its deep meaning and the unfathomable love it embodied.

What Yeshua had done was clear enough. The wisdom he carried in his "flesh" was diffused into the whole collective reality of humankind when his body hung on the tree (a Roman desecration of a sacred symbol, this hanging of criminals on the World Tree …).

He had also shown how anyone could be symbolically attuned to that great infusion of knowing and renewal of life, and this without the secrecy and expense of the other mystery cults in the Empire which offered salvation and union with their God (or Goddess). The "king's bounty" was truly available to all and at a far higher spiritual level than when his blood-spots on your clothing were a sacramental union with the Divine whose presence he had mediated.

The ideas of Christ came along the trade routes of the Roman Empire at first. There are many ideas about exactly when and exactly who, but their early arrival in Britannia is very likely as there had been a lucrative metal trade between South Western tribes and the Semitic peoples of the Mediterranean for many centuries before the Roman invasion. Tin from Cornwall had gone into Middle Eastern wargear for millennia, part of the bronze used everywhere before the secret of iron production escaped from the control of the Hittites … Tin was a strategic metal and the trade was heavily protected. This was one reason the Romans were so keen to take over the Carthaginian cities. Carthage controlled the flow of tin. So the Celts of the South and West were familiar with Phoenician and Judaean peoples (Carthage was a

Phoenician colony made good …). These folks brought ideas from the whole of the Middle East. The Celts were not an isolated culture.

Rome brought other things. More ideas, carried by its mercenary troops from all over the Empire but also a different kind of infrastructure and social organisation, designed to cultivate (and strip!) the assets of the new territories in a secure and peaceful manner. The brought towns, roads, new technology and an effective bureaucracy and centralised organisation. This peace and security enabled greater wealth and learning and came to be much valued. The towns, or "Vici", administered the countryside around them, the "Pagi", more or less to the benefit of both. The native peoples who lived in that country, the "pagani" or Countrymen, carried a long heritage of local lore and spirituality, from remnants of the old Megalithic cultures, through their own formal bonds with the land consummated in Celtic fashion, to the new useful ideas brought by the Roman invaders. They had always valued ideas and the new towns were fertile sources of these. Indeed, it was through the culture of the towns that Yeshua's ideas came. The Christian organisation saw itself as "Milites", Soldiers of God, an organised army fighting old ignorance and planting new ways in men's hearts: just as the Roman army had planted new ways in men's outer lives.

The world-view was much the same in both organisations. The powerful and popular chivalric mystery cult of Mithras, brought out of Persia by that same army, was a powerful rival organisation, working to similar ends. The Church fought hard against young Mithras and, in the process took on board many of his cult's methods, ideas and outer forms. This was natural enough. Yeshua had given them little guidance on how to organise community life. They had either to integrate his clear spiritual teachings into current cultural forms or to take aspects of those forms to assemble new means of expressing socially the "Kingdom of Heaven" that was beginning to appear in their hearts. They tried many approaches, a great flowering of different spirits and community which, in the end, had to be forcibly "pruned" in the interests of cohesion and political expediency. Some distressing history there … These were not major problems in Britain. At first, the Roman state provided the structure, the Church growing hidden in its cracks. Later, when legal, the Church grew in a more or less orthodox manner, an alternative to many other legally recognised cults. Later, it became predominant, especially among the educated and the town dwellers. The "pagani" were slower in taking it up – they had their own ways – but it did spread into the countryside.

When Roman rule in Britain collapsed a lot of the old Celtic ways re-established themselves. Not fully, of course, for damage was great and much was forgotten, but the spread of Christian ideas switched from the normal Church organisation to lines of teaching within Bardic and Royal lineages as was traditional and proper. At roughly the same time (about 400 AD) new ideas of "Spiritual Warriorhood" came out of Egypt. Anchorites had long gone into the desert to war with evil spirits to help communities using prayer and asceticism. Now many of them were Christians. Scorned at first, they soon took on a "Guru" status and attracted communities of pupils. Schools and hostelries grew up around them They became successful.

The idea spread westwards. The Church in Gaul allowed Martin of Tours to experiment with these new "Monasteries". They proved a fertile source of charismatic Christian teachers, some of them from Britain (which was by now embroiled in a nasty, slow conflict by which imbalances of power left by Rome's departure were being adjusted, mostly in favour of English immigrants once there as mercenaries to keep the peace …). These early "Celtic saints" brought the monastic method to western Britain and Ireland, where it took off rapidly and virtually eclipsed the remnants of the normal Church organisation. Its success seems to have followed from its close resemblance to normal Celtic social patterns. Each monastery was like an extended clan household under an "Ab" or spiritual father. Both royal households and bardic colleges had similar patterns. They were also decentralised. Each king, each saint or "Ab" was more or less independent and self-reliant. The Church hierarchy developing in the rest of Europe was irrelevant to these Celtic saints. The kind of culture that could support such a hierarchy had vanished with Rome. It is thus decentralised, learned monasticism which spread to convert the Irish, the Picts and even the Saxon Northumbrians. It even provided learned missionaries to serve the consolidation of the Roman Church in the Rhineland, but that's another story!

The Roman Church slowly reasserted its hierarchy across Britain after 600 AD. Mostly using Saxon and Norman military power, but that too is another story! A unique and mostly peaceful synthesis of Druid and Christian ideas was discarded.

Another important face of our salmon also emerged from the Middle East. The great Magian religion, spread all over the Indo-European world, was modified by Zoroaster in Iran and by Buddha in Northern India. Cosmic ideas from these sources filtered into Babylon and Chaldaea and fused with Egyptian star-lore to give the basis of Greek and Roman astrology. A part of the package of ideas contained the notion of the precession of the equinoxes, whose importance we will soon see. Another portion of this package told Magian sages exactly when and where to find the next Saviour predicted by their ancient faith (see the New Testament accounts of Yeshua's birth).

Yeshua came to shift the world from the Age of Aria to the Age of Pisces, according to this world-view. This cosmic role of the Christ earned him the title of the Great Fish in the 2nd century Church. The Celtic salmon, leaping into view from the pool of the deep underworld, could be seen to embody this idea also. There are many interesting images inherent in this wheel of world-ages or Aeons (*fig. 4*).

It is tempting to bring in the Great Lion-headed image of Zurvan, Endless Time. This portrayal of the spiritual meaning of the equinoctial precession was met with at the end of a sequence of initiations within Mithraism and would thus have been understood by many people (though to speak openly of it was forbidden!). Perhaps that great Aeon can serve as a reminder of the tremendous heritage of histories and ideas, from Indo-European as well as Hebrew sources, that Yeshua of Judea gathered in his capable hands and wove into a new garment for a whole new world. He was, after all, said to have been sent to everyone; not just the venerable Hebrew lineage he arose within.

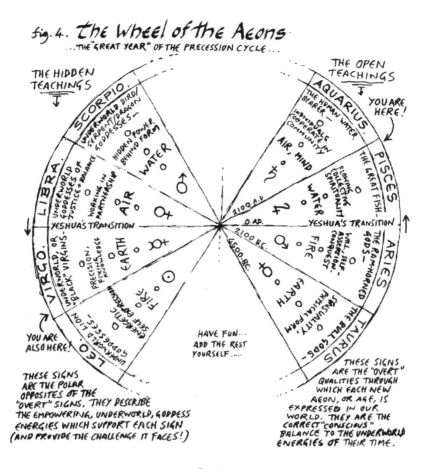

*fig. 4*

To bring this rambling serpent of a narrative back to Glastonbury, what was here before the Saxon king Ine built the first known abbey church? Surely Roman citizens, who were Christians at first, either local aristocrats or traders at the port (at Beckery and Northover) or at the settlement roughly where Benedict Street now is. Metalworkers, perhaps, as Roman slagheaps exist along Porchestall Drive. Later, when the kings reasserted themselves and the new Egyptian monastic ideas came by sea, a saint called something like "Kei" or "Tokei" may have set up a little community at "Lantokay" over the causeway in Street where the church is now." Llan Tokei" would have meant "the sacred enclosure of St Tokei". Perhaps it was built about 450 AD or so, some way from what remained of the little port. Perhaps, indeed, there was a "little wattle church" dating back to the earliest Christians still standing near the Benedict St. settlement where St. Mary's now is, more or less? It is around 450 AD to 500 AD that stories of anchorites coming here start to concentrate. Gildas, Bridget, Patrick, Collen etc. all refer to a simple monastic community in the area. A set of these little buildings appear atop the Tor – were these the cells for the anchorites from Llan Tokei? Did these anchorites proliferate and then settle at a college near the old church in the then decaying Roman settlement? Was this the "monastery" that Patrick organised and Bridget visited? Was it their remnant King Ine wished to honour with a new church when he became a Christian, married into the local royal line and took over the territory in the late 600's?

All is speculation, yet it is conspicuous that there is little or no record of violent transition in Glastonbury. The Salmon's Leap happened here in a remarkably pure and clear manner. The beauty of that coming forth and unfolding of life is worthy of careful meditation. And here the serpent's coils end. If you would learn more, sit in silence in the Abbey and the sacred land around it and see what arises in the peace of the heart.

*The Salmon's Leap is illustrated, perhaps, by a carving in Glastonbury Abbey – to the right of the High Altar, in the bottom of a recess between two windows of the 1340s retro-choir*

*Avalon Magazine, Issue 10, Autumn 1998*

# A MERMAID'S TALE

**Alan Royce** *suggests that there is much more to
the legendary Mermaid than we might realise.
So, where do mermaids come from?*

We have to exclude the likes of Selkies from this enquiry, as they are
remnants of ancient British ancestor cults and take us in a quite different direction. Sticking to the well-known carp-maiden hybrid, with
its penchant for song, mirror and comb, let us see what we can see.

A simple way of reading "mermaid" is as follows – and serves as a
convenient entry point to the labyrinth...

...the Mermaid as a symbol of the astro-
logical opposition of Virgo and Pisces

This has a Christian meaning, in that, at the time of Jesus' birth the
Vernal Equinox point was at the "Nodus" or knot in the cord
connecting the two fish of Pisces – that is, Jesus as the "Divine
Springtime/New Year".

The mermaid is also a fine emblem for the Age of Pisces which Jesus inaugurates – Pisces defining the Age's outer form (its "feet" which touch the earth, so to speak) and Virgo as its inner or spiritual quality (its "heart"). This Virgo/Pisces opposition resurfaces interestingly in the Gospel story of the five loaves and the two fishes.

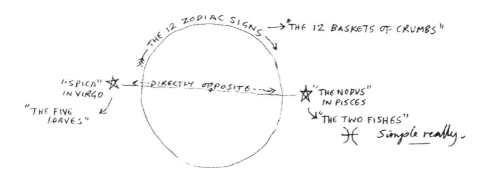

The five loaves are a subtle reference (...simple, really) in which the thinking is as follows:

The loaves feed 5000 men,
1000 is noted in Hebrew by large Aleph, Aleph in Greek is Alpha, "A",
5000 is therefore five Alphas,
Five Alphas in Greek is "Pentalpha",
Pentalpha = ✩ (... not so simple)

This star is not just Spica, the "Grain Star" in Virgo, it is also developed later as a glyph for the "five wounds of Christ" and is the form developed against the zodiac of the conjunctions of Venus and Sun over an eight-year period. This cycle was related to the idea of Sacred Kingship, and Christ was indeed considered a King of a Spiritual Kingdom.

This fish and grain symbolism is of ancient provenance in the Middle East, as we will find later. Meanwhile, an interesting comment upon this occurs in one of the old Merovingian centres in France – the

Merovingians having claimed some form of descent from Jesus as a variant of the normal Frankish royal custom of tracing pedigrees to a divine ancestor.

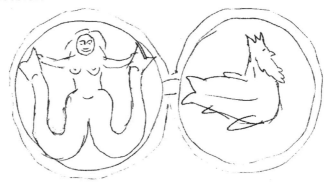

The Merovingian Mermaid wall paintings

Now, what have we here? The two-tailed mermaid certainly suggests Pisces and possesses a "Virgo" body, but what of the King with the single fishy body? Perhaps he is the royal star Fomalhaut – "Mouth of the Fish" which is the little constellation Piscis Austrinus (Southern Fish) which hides in the waters of Aquarius. This star is one of the "four holy watchers" which guarded the seasonal changes back when the Vernal Equinox was in Taurus.

Perhaps more relevantly, this constellation is considered the source, or parent, of the two fishes of Pisces. Could we suggest that the Southern Fish is Christ – the Great Fish – as source, and the Pisces/Virgo pairing is Christ's revelation, his "spiritual feeding" of his human following, the "Ekklesia" esoterically rep-resented in Christian Gnosticism as the Magdalene, the one who fully received Christ's revelation...? Mary Magdalene's imagery and gematria abounds in fishy symbolism – witness the works of Margaret Starbird. However, that is enough of this recent history. It may help to look at earlier mermaids...

We need to digress here to give a little background and speak of mighty Inanna/Ishtar and Enki/Ea. The reasons for this detour will emerge from the waters of chaos as we progress. First, we must delineate the three roads in the sky and show how they link to the land and the primary Gods of Mesopotamia.

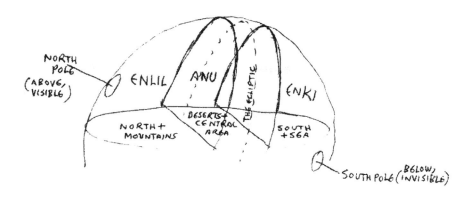

This is a table of these relationships:

| GODS | PLACES | SKY |
|---|---|---|
| **ENLIL**<br>[Lord Wind]<br>Ruler of fate and storms | Northern Mesopotamia and mountains | Northern sky and polar stars which do not set |
| **ANU**<br>[Heaven or Heaven's River]<br>All-Father of Gods | Central Mesopotamia<br>Deserts<br>The two rivers | A band of sky each side of ecliptic (approx. overhead),<br>path of sun, moon, planets |
| **ENKI**<br>[Lord Earth]<br>Wise helper of humankind<br>Ruler of waters | Southern Mesopotamia<br>River mouths and sea | Southern sky and "stars in the waters below the earth" |

Enki is of most interest to us here as he rules earth (KI) and the waters below the earth (ABZU or APSU). His stars daily descend into the Southern underworld, and such descents are common in Enki's mythology. He descends into the Underworld to bring back the New for those who live on his Earth.

169

The tale of Inanna's descent into the great below is too famous for us to go into here – suffice it to say that Enki rescues her, being an expert in Descent and the Great Below.

More useful to our thread is the tale of the Huluppu Tree. This curious botanical was brought up by Enki from the Great Below, and ended up floating down the Euphrates. It was washed up near Inanna's palace and planted in her gardens by her retainers. She wished to use it to make the throne and bed which were emblems of her city's power, but discovered that it was already in use – in its branches the Stormbird cared for its chicks, in its trunk Lilith had her house, and a great serpent coiled among its roots. She was distressed in being thwarted in this way and called in Gilgamesh to sort out the problem for her. He killed the serpent and drove out the other inhabitants – the Stormbird to the Northern mountains, Lilith to the desert regions. In gratitude Inanna made "emblems of Kingship" for him from the roots (the Rod and Ring common in art at the time, perhaps?) and then had her throne and bed made of the trunk and branches.

What we seem to have here is an older religious pattern, sourced by Enki from the hidden spiritual reservoirs of the Underworld, being replaced by Enki's daughter (or successor) Inanna by a pattern more relevant to her city state.

Note what the old system contained:

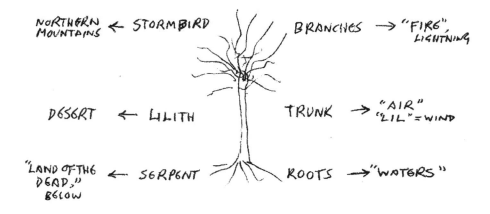

This system is interesting in that it reflects both the cosmos (sky, land, waters) and Lilith, as a human figure, suggests the tree as a microcosm of some kind. We will develop this female image of the cosmos later; first, let us see the earliest images of mermaids and mermen from this same culture.

Sumerian merman, one of a commonly-portrayed mythic race linked, for obvious reasons, to Enki as ruler of land & water. Note the resemblance to our Merovingian Fisher King

In later, Babylonian, times Enki himself becomes the fish-tailed teacher who emerges from the deep to teach spiritual and cultural things to his beloved humans. He continues into the figures of Oannes and even Dagon – whose name in fact means "grain" rather than "fish", but who was considered a fish deity in later antiquity.

Back, however, to our wind-maiden Lilith. She, as "Air" or "Breath", is a mediator between the Northern stars/Above and the Southern Stars/Below, breath between fire and water. She is, at one and the same time, an image of microcosm and macrocosm, body and cosmos. She develops, in time, into the Divine Sophia, the female image of soul and world-soul, but she passes through other forms which are interesting.

Her later, Western, Semitic form can be exemplified by Atargatis or Derceto (Greek forms of a Semitic word something like Tarkhu) who has a rich mythology in which she manifests through forms such as Dove, Fish and Grain. Semiramis, the great Builder-Queen of Mesopotamia, is said to have been her daughter – which would make her a Goddess of city and culture.

Another form appears in early images of Artemis, Our Lady of the Beasts, in the Hyksos- and Phoenician-influenced early Aegean and Anatolia.

BOEOTIA 700 BCE,

Bee's head & birds "Above" Sky – honey is considered compatible with fire.
"Beasts" Bull & horn? The Land – Aleph is an ox's head.
Fish & dogs Underworld Creatures – "fish & net" theme recurs in Mary Magdalen imagery.

A roughly-contemporary Artemis image from Italy, 800 BCE, keeps the themes of symmetry and the three levels, with an interesting hint.

Wings = Above, Sky.
Hands & beasts = Centre, Land.
Skirt + net = Below, Waters

But note: The big cats are Lion and Puma, the beasts of Apollo and Dionysos respectively. Apollo is Artemis' twin, also born to Leto (with Artemis' help). Dionysos is her hunting companion.

This suggests a structure a bit like this:

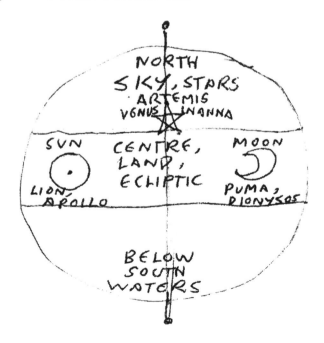

Or even, with reference to the *Three Mothers* article, like this:

This structure is reflected in curious places. Here are a few examples from varying periods in a middle Eastern context:

A Mithraic lead plaque

Birds at the top, men and beasts at the centre, the Underworld Mithraic cave with a sacred meal at the base.

174

Note: The combination of the central Mithras figure and the table below are quite like our Artemis image; Artemis as Hekate may have served as a Sophia-type presence in the cult.

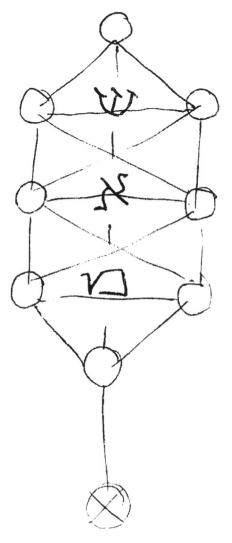

**The Mother letters in the Tree of Life -**

ש = SHIN, FIRE, HEAD

א = ALEPH, AIR, CHEST

מ = MEM, WATER, BELLY

Air mediates between fire and water, hence the letters can be also:-

ש   SUMMER
     SPIRIT, NOUS

א   SPRING/AUTUMN
     SOUL, PSYCHE

מ   WINTER
     BODY, PHYSIS

We can also use the same thinking to obtain:

| | | | |
|---|---|---|---|
| FIRE | ADAM "SPIRIT" | MARY MAGDALENE [Tower, Doves] Sky? | DOVE OF HOLY SPIRIT |
| AIR | EVE "SOUL" | MARY OF BETHLEHEM [House of Bread] Virgo?  Land? | JESUS and JOHN the BAPTIST |
| WATER | SERPENT "BODY/SENSES " | MARY OF BETHANY (BE IT HA NUN) [House of the Fish] Pisces?  Waters? | THE JORDAN |

We now have an interesting set of insights into the patterns folded within our two types of mermaid – the "Enki" figure who brings forth new spiritual realities from the Void, and the "Inanna" or "Lilith" type who receives and mediates and embodies these truths. This is the true Hierosgamos, the Sacred Marriage, which some consider Jesus and Mary Magdalene to have enacted. As can be seen, it is a thing of spirit and there is no requirement for a physical consummation. Similar enactments can be detected in the interactions between Moses and his sister Miriam, or the Bab and his disciple Tahirih... or indeed, the Divine Impulse and any one of us.

So next time you encounter our "little mermaid", remember her ancient and honourable lineage and the secrets woven into her familiar form.

*Avalon Magazine, Issue 32, Spring 2006*

# ROOTS OF THE RUNE TREE

*Alan Royce tracks the ancestry and heritage of the Runes.*

A wise old priest once taught me this: "The forces of magic are universal, but they need a specific local vehicle in which to work." He was right, for the magic of the Somerset Levels is rather different from that of the Essex marshes of my own childhood.

It is not so much that Somerset is 'Celtic' and Essex 'Saxon' – there are Celts in the land in Essex, and the language of Somerset (indeed, even its name) is very Saxon indeed. It is more to do with the fact that Somerset is a part of the ancient Atlantic Trade culture which linked Ireland and Western Britain to Brittany, Spain, North Africa and the Mediterranean, while Essex is a part of the equally-ancient Baltic Trade culture, which links Eastern Britain with Belgium, France, Denmark, Sweden, Norway, the Baltic States, and all parts of Central Europe and Asia accessible by the great rivers which empty into these seas.

Put even more simply – Somerset is Tarot Country, while Essex prefers Runes... which leads me more or less clumsily into my present ramble.

Now, the Runes are a bit of a puzzle. You can buy books on them full of esoteric lore, colours, dates, meanings, trees, herbs. You can buy books detailing their ancient connections to Goddess lore or to Shamanism. However, if you want to seek out actual evidence for any of this, you will find frighteningly little. There are numerous inscriptions on stone and metal and other durable materials, some of which are obviously encryptions or magical sound or number sequences. There are 'Book Runes' used, reasonably enough, to write things in books. There are a few poems in which Runes stand for (mostly Saxon) words. There are also three or four poems which purport to be commentaries on Runic meanings. And that is about it.

All the rest is from 'Tradition' or 'Speculation' – both good, useful magical techniques, but usually only relevant for the individual or a like-minded audience.

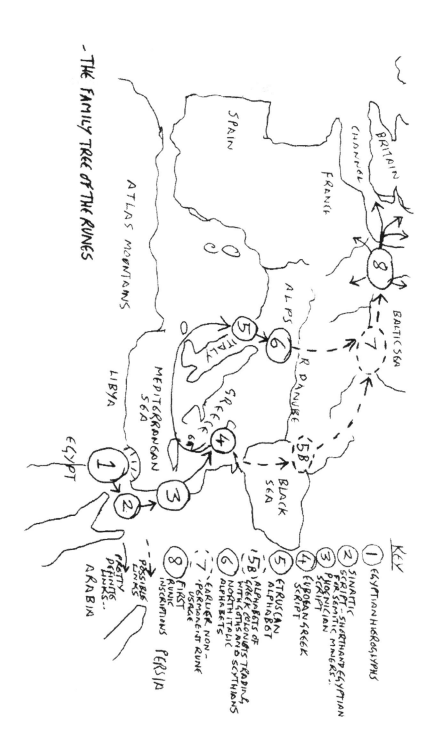

THE FAMILY TREE OF THE RUNES

KEY

1) EGYPTIAN HIEROGLYPHS
2) SINAITIC SCRIPT – SHORTHAND EGYPTIAN FOR SEMITIC MINERS...
3) PHOENICIAN SCRIPT
4) EUROPEAN GREEK SCRIPT
5) ETRUSCAN ALPHABET
5B) ALPHABETS OF GREEK COLONISTS TRADING WITH GOTHS AND SCYTHIANS
6) NORTH ITALIC ALPHABETS
7) EARLIER NON-PERMANENT RUNE USAGE
8) FIRST RUNIC INSCRIPTIONS

- - - POSSIBLE LINKS
——— PRETTY DEFINITE LINKS...

The Runes present us with two basic problems:

1. Where do the letter-*forms* (or glyphs) come from?
2. Where does the letter *sequence* come from?

The relevance of the latter question becomes apparent when the former has been examined, as you will see.

The first 'proper' Runes appear somewhere in the second century or so CE in the general region of the busy trade route across southern Denmark, linking the Baltic peoples to the North Sea and the Rhine. The practice of cutting these letters into metal (as gold medals or Bracteates) and stone (as boundary or tombstone/memorial inscriptions) seems to have been brought home by "Danish" lads who served in the Roman armies as auxiliary troops. The letters themselves could have come from this trade route or perhaps from further East. This is not clear, as there are gaps in the archaeology. What is reasonably clear is their ancestry:

To go into these transformations in detail would be complex and tedious. However, a simple comparison of Phoenician, Greek and Runic will make my point about the 'problem' of the letter sequence.

As can easily be seen, the Greek and Phoenician scripts follow a rather similar letter order – a sequence which in fact evolved into that of Latin script and thence to our own. The Runes, on the other hand, show a different sequence entirely. This brings us neatly to our second problem. Where does this sequence come from? If those who formed the Runes merely wanted an alphabet, why not just copy the Greek, Etruscan or Latin models available to them? What was so important about this particular letter order? Well, there are some clues.

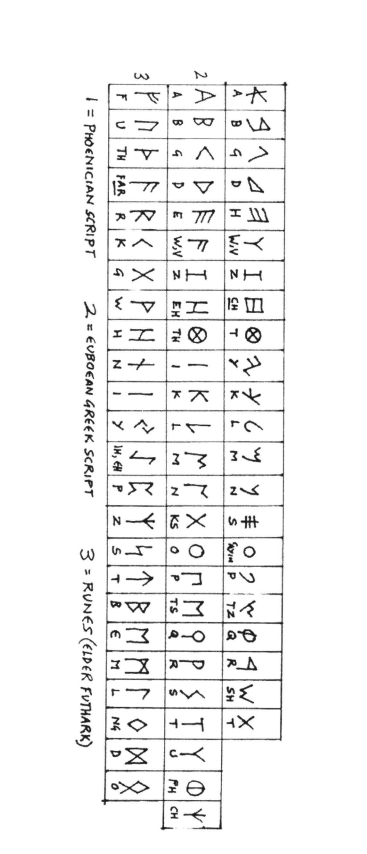

1 = PHOENICIAN SCRIPT  2 = EUBOEAN GREEK SCRIPT  3 = RUNES (ELDER FUTHARK)

First, the letters have meaningful names – "cattle", "wild ox" etc. Second, the Rune row is broken into thirds (this could be a copy of Greek, or it could have another meaning). Third, many Runic inscriptions were written in serpentine form, or inside the bodies of carved serpents. Fourth, some of the names of letters are what we call 'Gods' (an oversimplification of the ancient view of these things).

Indeed, to have a chance of solving our puzzle, we need to fit ancient eyes into our modern heads. Where will we find a serpent, often divided into thirds, which contains a fixed procession of signs, some of which represent Gods? To ancient eyes the answer was plainly visible every night. It is the living presence of the Ocean Stream which surrounds the solid disk of the Earth, a watery stream which extends out into the realm of the stars.

The 'serpent' here has two forms. One circles with this ocean, the other hangs coiled about the pole, writhing between the Bears (or Oxen) which guard and turn it. For the more esoterically-minded, these serpents lived on any horizon and in the spine of the one who observed it. But this goes too far from our path...

The great serpent Jormungand, child of Loki and Angrboda, is the Norse version of this cosmology. There are esoteric levels here too.

So, could the Runes be the starry 'bones' of this great serpent, a series of divisions of either the zodiac (as twenty-four halves of the sidereal zodiac signs), or of the celestial equator (as hours of right ascension)? An interesting notion. But starting where? Our first clue may help. Which zodiac sign could be signified by the terms 'cattle' or 'wild ox'? Not hard – it has to be Taurus, the Great Bull of Heaven. Now, in which direction are we travelling? The third Rune is the clue – an 'opposing giant'. 'Giant' comes from the Greek 'gigantes' or 'earth-born'. Is there a giant opposing Taurus from below the celestial equator/ horizon?  Indeed there is, and his name is Orion.

Our beginning then looks like this:

This suggests that 'cattle' is the same as 'Pleiades' in this scheme.

Let us stay with this for a while. We could continue this pattern round the zodiac to see how it fits, but I would like to digress here a little. At the time when the Runic letters were placed in this pattern, circa 200 CE or earlier, the spring equinox was around the Nodus, the knot in the cord linking the two fishes of Pisces. A couple of thousand years earlier, the spring equinox was around the area of the Pleiades. The pattern could have been in use long before the useful new Etruscan letters were used to decorate its parts. But where?

Our Baltic traders would have sold amber across Europe, to both Etruscans and Greeks. They probably had contacts along the Danube, which both amber routes had to cross. The Danube carried trade from the Black Sea and further East. Do we see signs of our pattern in this direction, say among Scythians, Persians, or even Vedic Indians? We do indeed, and the Vedic version gives us another important clue to its use – the primacy of the Moon.

If you are a nomadic, or forest-dwelling, people, then stable horizons are not a big part of your worldview. You can't make much use of the rising and setting points of the sun to mark your seasons, and even the subtle trick of measuring midday shadows is not very reliable. How then do you make a calendar?

Well, you consult the moon and the stars. Those with eyes to see, and clear night skies, will note that the moon takes about twenty-seven days to move through all the available stars stretched around the ecliptic. It is not a major jump to divide the ecliptic into twenty-seven parts representing these days, and a bit of poetic licence gives us Chandra the Moon God who spends each night with one of his Starry Wives in unending sequence. The homes of these Star-Wives are called Nakshatras or Lunar Mansions. A bit more intelligence in the observer and it is noted that the Full Moon happens at a point on the ecliptic directly opposite the point which the Sun happens to occupy.

The Vedic folk were no fools. Their old lunar months were named for the place where the full moon was to be found at a particular solar season.

For instance, the month Kãrttika is when the full moon is in the mansion called Krittikã, and the sun is opposite in one called Vishãkhã. The wheel will, one hopes, make this important relationship reasonably clear.

Conveniently for us, at the time when the Runes were composed the Tropical, or Seasonal, Zodiac and the Sidereal Zodiac more-or-less coincided, so the diagram gives the situation at that time. All we need to do is to add the Runes at their stations around the zodiac, to see what happens. And what happens is interesting, especially when it comes to the Runes Tyr (which looks like an upward-pointing arrow) and Eh (which looks like a capital M).

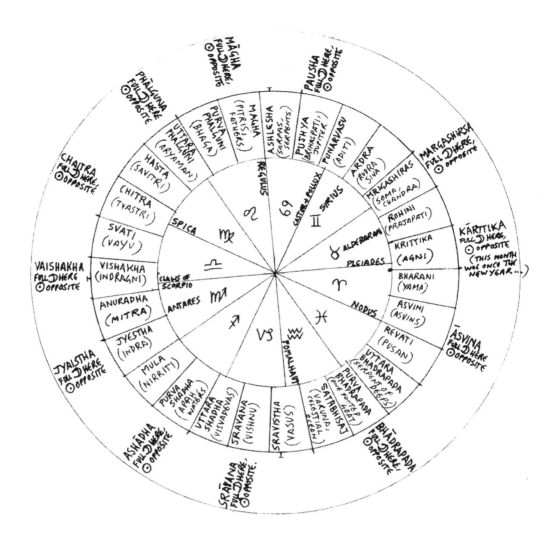

The Vedic Lunar Mansions compared with the Sidereal Zodiac. The outer ring gives the lunar months – their positions are approximate as full moons do not always occur in the same spot. Some important stars have been included.

185

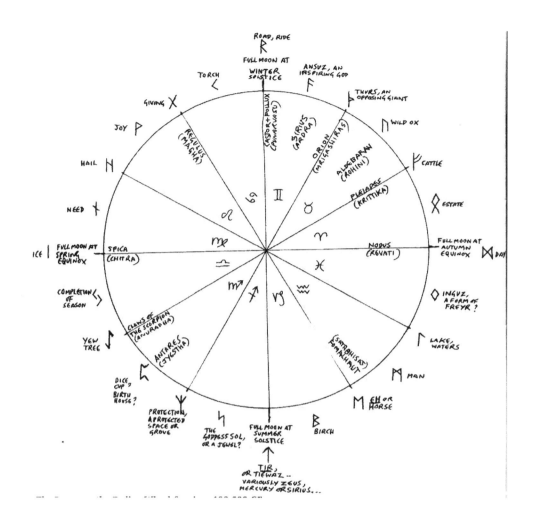

### The Runes on the Zodiac Wheel for circa 100-200 CE.

Staying with the idea of full moons in star groups, we find the positions of Tyr and Eh bracket the likely periods in which Sirius could be observed to rise just before the sun at dawn (the further North you are, the later this is in this period). TYR is the Full Moon on the Sagittarius/Capricorn cusp at Midsummer, Eh is the full moon a month further on, when the sun is conjunct Regulus – the marker of the rising of Sirius in our own latitudes.

The name Tyr may be a corruption of Tishya – a Vedic archer identified with Sirius (and the Pushya mansion) or of Tishtrya, a Persian form of Sirius who takes the form of a white horse to battle the demon of drought in the form of a black horse. This battle caused the yearly rains to come, so Sirius/Tishtrya was considered the 'water star'. Compare the role of Isis as Sirius in Egypt – herald of the yearly Nile flood... all a part of the same weather system in that region.

So Tyr and Eh could both be Sirius markers, a notion supported by an Arab traveller who spoke of Sirius being one of the Gods worshipped in Gotland in his time (early Middle Ages).

Well, this use of the Runes as the stars forming a backdrop to the Full Moons of the year shows promise. But is the Vedic system not rather distant from the Baltic and the Jutland trade corridor?

Let us add some plausible intermediary forms. There are numerous common themes here. The Autumn-period new years, based on Full Moons in the region of the Pleiades or Aldebaran, tend to be associated with feasts of the old Light-God Mitra, bull sacrifices and sacred beverages. In Gaulish times, a God the Romans called Mars Meduris presided: a neat fusion of Mitra and Medua, which means intoxication.

The sun/full moon pairings across the zodiac carry many themes as well. There is a whole complex of ideas around the Sagittarius/Gemini opposition involving waters, archers, the underworld (below-ecliptic Sirius), Apollo, and the Moon as huntress. These pairings were important in classical religions, and bear much meditation.

There is even a hint of an answer to a problem in the modern study of Runes... does the sequence start with 'cattle' or with 'wild ox'? Given that Aldebran was a major season-marking star, and that the later Persian Kings shifted to a solar calendar whose year started at Spring equinox (Nõrooz), the sun in Taurus replaced the moon as season marker, and the year's start could be determined by the rising of the Pleiades just before the sun at dawn. So the cycle could begin with 'cattle' as the visible sign of Sun conjunct Aldebaran, or 'wild ox' as the conjunction itself – you could take your pick. 'Cattle' might suggest an outer, mundane viewpoint, 'wild ox' an inner, esoteric one.

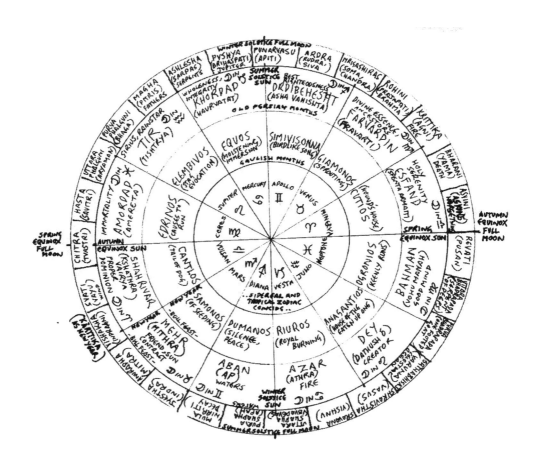

Old Persian and Gaulish (Coligny) Calendars compared to the Vedic Lunar Mansions

Well, this is rather a preliminary exposition of my pet theory. Feel free to expand it, destroy it, or make of it what you will. But above all, have fun in the process!

*Avalon Magazine, Issue 33, Summer 2006*

# THE MYSTERY OF MITHRAS

**Alan Royce** *investigates the cult of Mithras, its*
*origins and its influence on the modern world.*

Long ago, in a galaxy far, far away, I visited Newcastle upon Tyne on
a field trip to study techniques of rural regeneration. This was part of
an abortive attempt to become a Town Planner, and was so enthralling
that a friend and I found ourselves wandering around the local museum
looking at exhibits of material from Hadrian's Wall.

One of these exhibits was a reconstruction of a Mithraeum from one
of the big forts along that venerable Roman border defence. We looked
over the rail into this dim, cave-like chamber, with its side-benches
and stone altars and wall-paintings – and immediately and inexplicably
felt at home. The impression was so strong that I can feel it as I write
this.

But what, I wondered at the time, was a Mithraeum? Now, some twenty years later, I can perhaps go some way towards answering that question.

Plutarch writes that, around 100 BCE, Pompey's navy defeated "Cilician Pirates" in the eastern Mediterranean. Cilicia was an area of southern Turkey. The city of Tarsus (of biblical fame) was in Cilicia.

These pirates are said to have introduced the worship of Mithras to their Roman conquerors, a fine tale which may even be true, given the
early importance of the cult in Rome's port city of Ostia and the prominent presence of references to the Twin Brothers, the Dioscurii, who
were sons of Jupiter by Leto and were particular protectors of sailors.

The problem with this is that the earliest recognisable Mithraic imagery in Rome appears around 100 CE, well into the Christian period.
Some, indeed, have argued that Mithraism is a Pagan borrowing from
Christian ideas, while others have argued the precise opposite. A little
more of this later, perhaps.

First we need to give an idea of what a Mystery was, for Mithraism was one of many such at that time.

Ancient religions were not like those with which we are familiar today. Their goals were different. Most peoples had an official state cult whose function was to keep sweet the relations between that state or city and its ruling deity. This was achieved by pious observance of ancient customs, and careful attention to the instructions of the Gods via oracles, omens and dreams.

The public sacrifices were a major source of slaughtered meat in ancient cities and were shared in a hallowed manner between the Gods, their priests, and those attending the sacramental act. In private homes a lesser reflection of these sacrifices occurred, cheaper animals being offered to the spirits of the family and of their land. At the family level, the head of the family performed the rites. At the state level, official priesthoods did the work. There was considerable overlap in the Roman state between priesthoods and the role of senator, magistrate and decurion (an equivalent to our own councillors).

The imagery of the Sacrifice (and its Holy Victims), and the meals shared with the Gods, was all-pervasive. This shared meal in the Divine Presence is also at the core of Mithraism.

A Mystery was an addition to the state and domestic cults. Its purpose was to raise the spiritual state of individuals, in order to improve their life in the world and to gain them a friendly reception in the post-mortem realms. These were areas which the normal cults didn't really address.

Mysteries were built around a number of Divine Stories and varied accordingly, but they had in common the themes of a spiritual journey, emotive dramatisations, imparted secret knowledge (such as divine names, or passwords to divine gates), sacred objects to interact with, and a process of "divinisation" to undergo, in which the mortal candidate was given the purity and divine qualities to enable them to "meet the Gods face to face and worship them".

THE RAVEN IS APOLLO/SOL'S MESSENGER.

THE KNIFE MAY REPRESENT THE PLEIADES...

THE DOG - CANIS MINOR, THE SNAKE - HYDRA, THE SCORPION - SCORPIO...

MANY IDENTITIES HAVE BEEN SUGGESTED FOR MITHRAS AND THE BULL... MITHRAS AS THE NORTH POLE AND BULL AS URSA MAJOR WORKS AS WELL AS ANY...

DEOINVM LANTONS

A SKETCH OF THE TAUROCTONY IN THE MITHRAEUM AT NEWCASTLE MUSEUM....

MITHRAS STABS THE BULL SURROUNDED BY RAVEN, SCORPION, SNAKE AND LITTLE DOG. CAUTOPATES HOLDS HIS TORCH DOWN, CAUTES HOLDS HIS UP, SOL AND LUNA LOOK DOWN FROM ABOVE...

191

There is much debate as to the particular stories around which Mithraism is built. The God Mithras is considered by some to be an evolution of an earlier Persian and Vedic God of Light, Truth, Contracts, and Wealth (in the form of cattle). This is supported by contemporary references to the cult as a "Persian Mystery", reflecting what were felt to be the practices of the Persian priestly caste, the Magi (source of the "Three Kings" in the Gospel tale, and of the term "Magic").

Others, however, consider the cult to be a mystery pattern deliberately composed in the Roman world to honour, perhaps, the royal cult of the Kings at Commagene (a country in Syria) or the memory of the Divine Alexander, conqueror of Persia and son of Ammon. This debate may continue for some time, for the simple reason that Mithraism contended with Christianity for the role of State Religion of the Roman Empire, and lost.

All that remains of Mithraism is a good deal of ruined architecture, damaged images, some enigmatic inscriptions and a number of literary references. There are no Mithraic scriptures, no books of common prayer. All must be reconstructed from fragments, as dinosaurs are constructed from fossilised bones. And as with dinosaurs, the priorities and assumptions current in science can make huge differences in the reconstructions produced.

With Mithraism, as with dinosaurs, the context is as important as the fragments themselves. The context is a system of state cults in crisis, as the known world expands and ideas diversify and mix along the trade routes. The context is also a plethora of competing systems claiming to "save" individuals from a chaotic life and a dismal afterlife as a shade in Hades' realm. The emphasis in religion in general was on correct observance of traditional acts rather than on morality or spiritual insight, an attitude which persisted to some extent within the "saving dramas" of mysteries. However, the context also included philosophers and theurgists who treated the ancient stories as metaphors to guide the soul towards perfection and immortality, so this kind of depth is not impossible within Mithraism. The Emperor Julian the Apostate was an initiated Mithraean and strongly suggests such depths in the clues left in his writings.

Not all Mithraic initiates were of Julian's calibre, however. Most were merchants, military men, and various kinds of administrators – the sort of folk who kept the empire in working order, and whose work moved them around. Ports and military centres figure strongly; in Ostia, Mithraeums are found in the palace, in wealthy homes, in buildings to do with trade guilds. In Britain, they turn up in London, York, and along the wall which kept out the Picts. To a rather limited degree, Mithraism could be considered a Freemasonry of its time and culture.

So, what is a Mithraeum like? Put simply: a long, often vaulted, room with an off-centre entry at one end and an apse or alcove at the other. The area near the entrance is often bare, but the rest of the room tends to have broad benches along both walls. These can serve as seats or as places for people to recline as at a formal Roman meal or at a Symposium (an event at which wine and philosophy were shared). The apse would have formed the "top table", so to speak, of a three-sided dining area. Images showing just such a "top table", with divine figures reclining at leisure, have been found in apses. These images show various attendants bearing rods or jars or fruits, and sometimes wearing masks, framing two central figures holding a drinking-horn and a bunch of grapes. Wine-mixing bowls (craters) and little tables bearing loaves like "hot cross buns" also appear.

A sacramental meal of wine and bread? Apparently so, as Christians made the curious argument that the Devil had caused Mithraism to produce a parody of the Eucharistic meal before Jesus had revealed it. This, of course, supports the story of Pompey's sailors introducing Mithraism before Jesus's time.

Did the two Mysteries borrow from each other? Maybe so, but they could equally have arisen from a common cultural background, side by side. Jesus, after all, would have begun with the language and concepts of his day, however much he transformed them later.

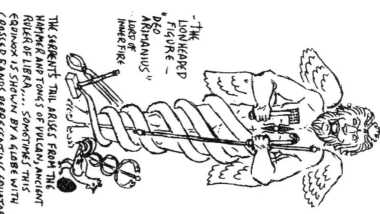

- THE LION HEADED "FIGURE" - DEO ARIMANIUS" - LORD OF INNER FIRE

THE SERPENT'S TAIL ARISES FROM THE HAMMER AND TONGS OF VULCAN, ANCIENT RULER OF LIBRA,... SOMETIMES THIS EQUINOX IS SHOWN BY A GLOBE WITH CROSSED BANDS REPRESENTING EQUATOR AND ECLIPTIC. THE ROD IS SATURN'S SYMBOL, HIS HEART THUNDERBOLT IS JUPITER'S, THE KEYS ARE TO INNER AND OUTER DOORS AND THE WINGS OFTEN BEAR SEASONAL EMBLEMS...

THE RITUAL MEAL IN THE MITHRAEUM... A SYMBOLIC RENDERING OF THE MEAL — THE CHARACTERS ARE LIKELY TO BE, FROM LEFT TO RIGHT, RAVEN, PERSES, PATER, HELIODROMUS, MILES, LEO. PATER AND HELIODROMUS RECLINE UPON THE SKIN OF THE SLAIN BULL WITH DRINKING HORN AND GRAPES. NOTE THE TABLE WITH FOUR "HOT CROSS BUNS"

THE ROCKBIRTH OF MITHRAS... A VERSION ON HADRIAN'S WALL PLACES THE "ROCK" AT THE CUSP OF CAPRICORN AND AQUARIUS, THE KNIFE COVERS TAURUS-GEMINI, THE TORCH COVERS VIRGO-LIBRA...

But what did Mithraists do, apart from sharing a meal? Well, for a start, there were seven levels or modes of membership. We have their names and a lot of associated imagery, and the arrangement of that imagery in the form of a sequence or ladder.

The first grades were considered "attendants" at the rites, the later grades were considered "participants". There are also many images of people in theatrical and religious stances of the day – people in small groups, performing rituals involving nudity, recitations, props. There are other images showing divine or mythic events recognisable from known literature.

Interestingly, the two categories overlap to some extent. Some of the divine acts portrayed were imitated by human participants in the Mithraeum. The impression is one of people taking on divine qualities by taking part in and experiencing divine events. Further than this, there is evidence that the inner, or metaphorical, meaning of these events was worked with. A member of the "Pater" grade, who ran the Mithraeum, refers to Mithras carrying a young bull "on his golden shoulders", and to the fact that this bull had been passed onto the writer's shoulders. This suggests that the bull is a symbol of the tradition or of the Mithraeum as a ritual group (much as a church is said to be the people gathered rather than the building).

Just as some churches are ornate and full of story-images, while others are plain and basic, so it was with Mithraea. The images the participants loved and worked with did not all need to be present on the walls, for they would be present in the actions and minds of the participants even in the simplest space.

Two great themes are reasonably constant; Astrology and the Tauroctony (Bull-slaying). Porphyry of Tyre and others say that the Mithraeum represents the cosmos with its moving stars and planets, its sun and moon. This cosmos is a cave, as in Homer's (and Porphyry's) cave of the Nymphs, and Plato's famous allegory – a limited space known to limited beings. Mithras is the one who is the Way out of the Cave to the bright realm of the Gods. This reflects the Hellenic notion of the "Sensible World" – the orderly physical realm our senses can apprehend – and the "Intelligible World" which is only perceptible to the developed intellect. The stars at that time were seen as purified souls, mediating the light of the "Intelligible" divine world into our dark cave of a cosmos. These, and lesser, souls, were the "Daemons" who bore divine influences from the heavens to the earthly realm. These influences were focussed through the "sensible" sun (Helios) via his seven rays (the planets).

Just as the stars mediated "Intelligible" divine light into "Sensible" form, so did the "Sensible" face of the sun mediate an "Intelligible" sun's power. This was the "Sun behind the Sun" or the "Sun at Midnight" often mentioned in Mystery contexts.

The connections between this "inner sun" and the "outer sun" seem to have been complex, and to have involved the Pleiades, Ursa Major, and perhaps other constellations held to possess seven stars... these sevens perhaps being seen as the higher octaves of the seven planets. In a Graeco-Egyptian magical papyrus, a spell has been found which has come to be called the "Mithras Liturgy". This spell is in fact a means to obtain an oracular contact with Mithras, and involves an inner journey from one's bodily elements to a being who is master of the inner fire (the lion-headed Deo Arimanius) and thence to the presence of Helios, who opens the way through his disk to a sevenfold gateway made of seven asp-headed maidens (the Pleiades) and seven bull-headed youths (Ursa Major).This gateway gives access to "the Supreme God Mithras", apparently via the polar void (there was no pole star at that time).

This journey may well be a simplified summary of a Way an initiate of the cult would follow in much more detail – a journey from Time and Form to the timeless and formless source, followed by a return with oracular "treasures". Perhaps this was a journey made again and again in the Mithraeum, transforming the initiate by steady increments through enactments, vows and contemplations, in order both to "deify" him and to prepare him for when he would make the journey for real as a post-mortem experience.

Why, you may ask, should one seek to understand this ancient spiritual path? Was it not superseded by Christianity? Well, one reason is that it holds up a kind of mirror to early Christianity. The Mithraic process of "deification" is very similar to what the early church termed "theosis", a process of perfection by means of outer observance and inner prayer which leaves the practitioner in a state capable of radiating divine qualities from their cleansed heart into the human world. This path was once considered a duty for all Christians, be they married householder or celibate monk.

Also, Mithraism is not actually dead...!

There are numerous groups and individuals who feel moved to work with this ancient road to the "source of the stars". Their approaches range from the comic via the magical to the deeply intellectual and academic. No-one as yet has a comprehensive understanding, but the diverse currents of research and experimentation may yet produce a new Mithraism for this time – a time just as troubled and turbulent as the decline of Rome.

*Avalon Magazine. Issue 35, Spring 2007*

# THE SERPENT IN THE BOWL

**Alan Royce** *offers new insights as to how artefacts such as the Gundestrup cauldron, and landscapes such as the 'earth cauldron' of Glastonbury, may have been understood and used by the ancient peoples.*

Since I moved to Glastonbury in the 1990s, I have been gently pushing away at the skin of the place to feel what is underneath. The mottled skin of 'New Age', 'Mainstream' and 'Youth' culture, and the tissues of Christian history and legend, are easy enough to find (indeed, one is immersed in them ninety per cent of the time) but I am after the bones on which the rest is hung. If you learn what pertains to the modern layers, then alter the focus of your inner and outer eyes to see past them, the deeper patterns begin to stand out.

But there is a problem. The folk who lived these patterns neither spoke nor lived as we do, and the only way to hear their voices and read their traces is to get as near to their worldview as you can.

Now the Somerset Levels and the areas around abound with Roman, Celtic and earlier landscapes, and more of these are uncovered and understood year by year. One pattern which appears is the considerable concentration of hill-forts around the Levels, plus the late Romano-Celtic temples which local dignitaries caused to be built on those same sites in the third and fourth centuries CE. This concentration suggests that the Levels, with their seasonal pools and peat bogs, were considered a sacred area. Two factors in this might have been the presence of several tribal boundaries in the area, and the important trade route between the Severn Shore communities and Poole Harbour (earlier Hengistbury Head) and the continent. The factor I'll concentrate on is the Levels themselves. Imagine a huge cauldron with sacred points around its rim, and you begin to form the image. A wonderful example of this image is the famous Gundestrup Cauldron – but more of this later.

First I must tell you a story, which you must believe or not as you will.

Before I moved here, at the request of certain powers of the land, I once went with friends to Norfolk to help renegotiate an agreement between them about a line of energy in the landscape and its use. While there, I had the opportunity to visit a Bronze Age burial mound and consult with its inmate. This venerable gentleman showed me, with every indication of revealing a hugely important and basic secret, a shallow brown bowl, full of water, set in his lap, in which swam a small and languid serpent.

As is normal in such contacts, this image meant almost nothing to me, and I dutifully and respectfully recorded it and hoped it would unfold in the future.

About fifteen years later, it is beginning to do so. So before I bring in the silver cauldron I have to speak on the Snake in the Waters. We need some basic notions here. In ancient cosmologies, water is the fluid life of the visible worlds, and fire is the divine energy which is its source. Flowing water is the circling of time and change – the 'Moving Image of Eternity', while the fiery light of the divine mind *is* that eternity. Any worldly phenomenon which combines water and heat is a reference to those two states – a harmonisation of opposites which can be seen in the hot spring, the cooking cauldron, the wine-mixing bowl, even the human body.

In its human form, this notion is elaborated for use in spiritual growth (the Mysteries) and in medicine.

This process of eating the world to make it a part of one's body and blood, then refining the spiritual fluids from this, then purifying these energies to store in the brain, were seen as the normal spiritual process of mankind. There were more-specialised 'fast-track' techniques, taught in the Mysteries and in Warrior societies, which involved the use of the pure energies concentrated in the genitals to make the seed of new humans. Think of Tantric sex and Taoist Yoga to get the general idea – although actual sex was not necessarily a part of the process.

Here is the general structure:

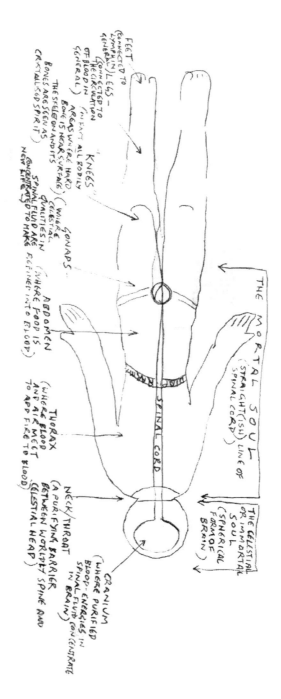

FEET
(CONNECTED TO
LYMPH IN LEGS -
GENERAL)

LEGS -
(CONNECTED TO
THE CIRCULATION
OF BLOOD IN
GENERAL)

KNEES
(IN FACT ALL BODILY
AREAS WHERE HARD,
BONE IS NEAR SURFACE.
THE SKELETON AND ITS
BONES ARE SEEN AS
CRYSTALISED SPIRIT.)

GONADS -
(WHERE
CELESTIAL,
SPINAL QUALITIES IN
SPINAL FLUID ARE
CONCENTRATED TO MAKE
NEW LIFE.)

ABDOMEN
(WHERE FOOD IS
REFINED INTO BLOOD)

THORAX
(WHERE BLOOD
AND AIR MEET
TO ADD FIRE TO BLOOD)

NECK/THROAT
(A PURIFYING BARRIER
BETWEEN WORLDLY SPINE AND
CELESTIAL HEAD)

CRANIUM
(WHERE PURIFIED
BLOOD-ENERGIES IN
SPINAL FLUID CONCENTRATE
IN BRAIN)

THE MORTAL SOUL
(STRAIGHT(ISH) LINE OF
SPINAL CORD)

THE CELESTIAL
OR IMMORTAL
SOUL
(SPHERICAL
FORM OF
BRAIN))

SPINAL CORD

200

But, before we digress into a dead end, we are now in a position to meet our Serpent in Water. Its head is the brain, its body the spinal cord, and after death its inner fire was felt to retain this form, and 'soul' (i.e. psyche) was thought to have the appearance of a serpent to those able to 'See'...

This 'Soulserpent' is our first key. The second is the zodiac, and the 'Melothesic Man'.

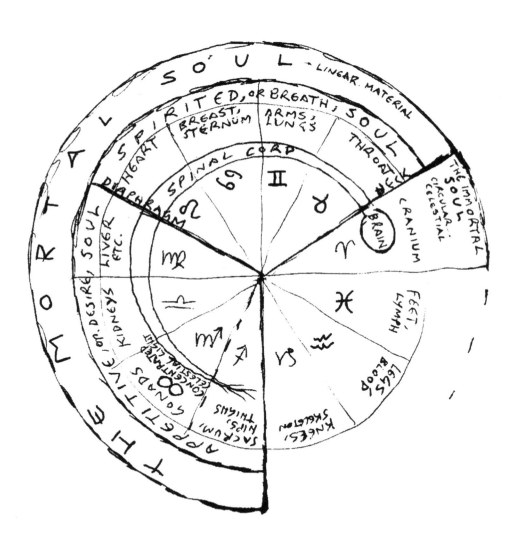

It should be apparent how the one fits into the other. It also becomes possible now to imagine the 'Worldsoul' as the serpent wrapped around the ecliptic (or equator) and to guess at the meaning of that enigmatic Celtic icon, the Ram-Horned Serpent.

And, having now been introduced to the Serpent, we should now bring in the Silver Bowl itself.

The Gundestrup Cauldron was found in a bog at Gundestrup in Denmark. It probably didn't come from there, and is likely to have been either war spoils or payment in precious metals for mercenaries It was found in a pile of fragments, having apparently been hacked apart for storage. This means that its original form is open to debate. I opt for the arrangement decided by one of its earliest investigators, based on the shape of rivet holes and solder marks, and ignoring the mysterious images on its inner and outer surfaces.

Our Ram-Horned 'Serpentsoul' features on this bowl in several places, as will be seen. I won't go into the months of puzzlement which led to my vision of this cauldron, I'll simply describe how I think it was used. You can then judge for yourself if you think my vision is useful.

The bowl is likely to date from about 100 BCE, so we can ignore Romano-Celtic religious practices. This means it was used in a sacred place open to the sky. As the Celtic day began at sunset, and the position of the moon against the stars defined months of the year, it is not too farfetched to imagine the wine/mead/blood-filled vessel being used as a Witch uses a cup of wine, to 'draw down' the moon's reflection and imbibe it during ritual. Our cauldron, though, could have been used to 'draw down' either moon or stars, thus distilling starlight from various constellations to attune with the various parts of the Melothesic Man and the 'Serpentsoul' in the body.

The following diagrams show how I think it would be done, and give the layout of the system as clearly as I can express it.

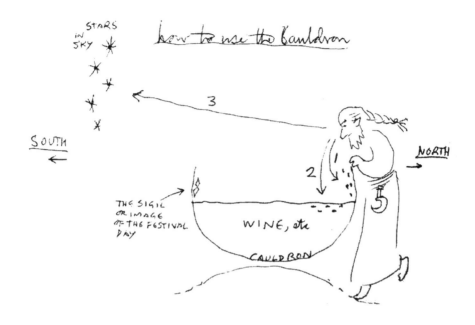

At midnight on the day of a festival – the sun is behind the Druid, below ground, in the North. The zodiac sign of that position of the sun, is immediately before him on the southern inner wall of the cauldron. (1) The sky opposite the sun-position, in reverse, is part of the cauldron wall in the North. (2) The Druid looks at the reversed *reflection* of this image in the 'wine' in the cauldron. (3) This is the same as the image conceived in the stars before him in the sky to the South. This method aligns the cauldron and magically unites cauldron, stars and Druid.

Important times/symbols in the cauldron are tripled – for example, the three bulls (starting at Samhain) and the three carnyx war-trumpet players (at Spring Equinox). This is interesting as it seems to emphasise the portion of the year from Spring Equinox to Samhain. Couple this with the fact that the vast majority of the human figures in the cauldron are in warrior costumes, and we have a strong hint that this item was a part of a Warrior-Kingship pattern of ritual. The period from March to October was the traditional time for military campaigning, cattle-raiding and the like – all the kind of activity which allowed the collection of sacred heads, the upgrading of warrior status, and the formation of the clientage relationships which held Celtic society together. Our bull-horned God holding on to the wheel is a form of the 'Celtic Mars' as the Romans would have called him, and the half wheel of seven segments is perhaps the seven star-signs of the war season. The bearded God holding it is probably Taranis, the Thunderer, controller of war in Lucan's text.

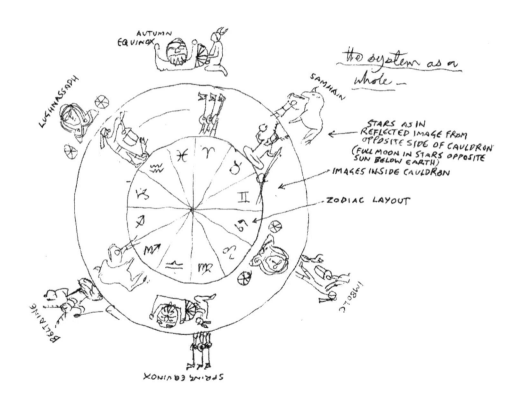

All that is consistent enough, but what happens if we map our cauldron's year onto the 'Melothistic Man'?

As can be seen, the war season neatly fits the part of the soul between head and belly. The gonadal region is where the Samhain bull sacrifice is performed, and the fruits of the soul-stuff concentrated in the gonads are harvested. The intriguing image of the ponytailed God inverting a man into a barrel (?), as Teutates is said to demand as sacrifice in Lucan, may relate to the 'blood soul' (Aquarius, legs, blood) and the 'soul in the head' in some manner Thus, all the soul-stuff is harvested outside the battle season. Is it collected *within* the battle season? Are we looking at a multi-levelled metaphor comparing war, the growth and harvesting of grain, and the growth and harvesting of the divine qualities in the individual all compressed into one complex visual tool?

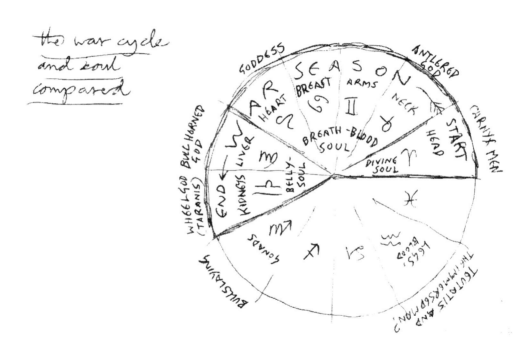

Is the warrior here a metaphor for the 'Serpentsoul'? The antlered God at Beltane suggests another layer here. He holds the ram-horned snake at its neck, and bears a torc (neck collar) – and the serpent has a round coil at the genital level. So far, so consistent, but his position on the wheel also relates him to the place where the Milky Way crosses the ecliptic, thus:

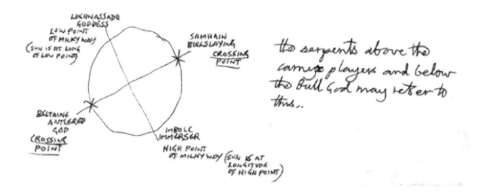

The serpents above the carnyx players and below the Bull God may relate to this.

Now, the Milky Way is also related to Souls. The souls which travel along it are often characterised as birds, rather than serpents. The fusion of these two concepts might be symbolised by a winged serpent (our dragon?), and the fact that these serpent and bird soul-circles meet at Beltane and Samhain, at neck and gonads, may have had a lot to do with the cult practices around heads and genitals. Perhaps the ancient and pure bird-soul ancestors were necessary for the serpent-souls in men to succeed in coming to fruition, and climbing out of the wheel of time to the timeless source-centre of the Polar stars.

As can be seen, there is a lot more work which could be done here, but this ancient metaphor uniting stars, body and time could be productively mapped onto the Somerset Levels (as 'cauldron') and the hills around (as 'cauldron rim'). The East-West 'snake' of the Polden Hills and the two 'gonads' of Glastonbury and Dundon are a strong hint.

The grain is ripe out there for the harvest, should anyone care to look beyond the confines of their own little house.

*Avalon Magazine, Issue 38, Spring 2008*

Blue Bowl – the latest news! This has been a subject that has refused to go away...

Assuming you have read the two 'Rose – themed' articles which cover our research these short comments should make sense.

Two major themes intrigued me; The Rose Stone Vigil and the Age of Michael.

The Vigil first then. It was conducted on the 12th September. What is special about that date? My long-term interest in Mithraism supplied the clue, and the answer is starlore. On the 12th of September in the early 1900s, the Sun reaches the longitude at the first stars in Krater, the Wine-Mixing Bowl below Leo. If you review the sunrise on that date you will see the heliacal rising of Regulus and know that, seeing from the west, the stars of Krater are 'buried in Chalice Hill'. This could be seen from the sluice in which Dr Goodchild hid the blue bowl and also from the tower of Chilton Priory on the Poldens where Catherine Maltwood left a sculpture which appears to refer to this very event!

Both she and Bligh Bond connect this event to the grail, or the two cruets, brought by Joseph of Arimathea. We think this is because of Jesus' likening his coming crucifixion to the 'Serpent upraised in the desert' and the early identification of this serpent with the stars of Draco hung upon the Royal Starcross, whose foot stood up on Regulus in Leo.

Joseph is quite early portrayed as catching the 'blood and waters' of the spear wound to Jesus' side in a cup (or other vessel). That is, he plays the 'Corvus' to the 'Krater' cup. The spiritual significance of this is that the Milky Way was seen as the rows of souls down into attachment to matter and back up again to source (the polestars) as they learnt detachment.

All the divine soul qualities were collected in the 'cup of mind' and the Crow (i.e. Corvus) represented one who has drunk of this cup and begun the re-assent to his timeless source.

Joseph of Arimathea symbolically conveys this gnosis to Glastonbury in the two cruets 'borne at his heart', or as the 'Rose Stone' in Bligh Bond's more alchemical allegory! That will suffice as a hint for those who want to put the local Joseph lore to good use.

Now for the age of Michael. The Abbot Johannes Trithemius, esteemed teacher of Agrippa and thus of later European Qabalists and magicians, wrote a little book about the sequence of planetary archangels who have ruled the world since its inception a few thousand years before Jesus. Each archangel ruled for, he felt, 354 years and then handed on to his (its?) successor. Last rulership would be that of Michael, the solar angel, and after that Jesus would return and all men would be judged. The angel before Michael was Gabriel, the Lunar archangel. The moon was felt to favour inner vision and secrecy and the sun to favour outer vision and openness. The Age of Gabriel ended in 1879 (or 1880 depending on how you calculated it!). These archangels and their terms of office were taken seriously by the more esoteric wing of the Establishment; witness the erection of that huge sundial gnomon, the Cleopatra's needle, in London on September 12th, 1878 (just to make sure it was ready!). The problem with the change over, though, was that all the practitioners involved, mostly male, were sworn to secrecy as befitted the previous Lunar age. How, then, could they give out their gnosis openly? A common answer to the problem was to employ women 'who had not been sworn to secrecy' as a channel. In practice this was combined with a strong interest in Polarity working and various kinds of 'co-Masonic' workings were employed. The most famous of these was the 'Hermetic Order of the Golden Dawn' set up in 1888 by the 'Societas Rosicruciana in Anglia', a research order for Master Masons. Most of the protagonists in the blue bowl story where either members of this august body or strongly linked to members thereof.

This call to openness of the Michael Age is one motive behind Dr Goodchild's 'Bowl' enactment. This is made clear from his writings and from the service-books which were used with the bowl in its

Bristol Oratory. These books also refer to a Golden Dawn. Further support comes from the 'ruby and cross and gold chain' Goodchild claims to have put in the bowl when he placed it into the sluice. 'Ruby Rose and Cross of Gold' is a translation of the Latin name of the inner order of the Golden Dawn. You can see how this relates to Bond's 'Rose' stone vigil also.

This esoteric starlore and calendar lore caused us all sorts of bother but we chased it down in the end! Given how much effort has been put into the Gabriel – Michael transition one wonders what is planned for when Jesus returns at the end of Michael's age, circa 2233CE.

All of this digging into the motivations behind the local 'blue bowl' lore also gave us the source of the Isis/Pan workings popularised by Dion Fortune's novels and the huge Michael emphasis of much New-Age material, but I'll leave you to dig that web of connections out for yourselves.

My own interests have headed off in slightly different directions – a combination of researching the mindset behind Mithraic Art and ongoing work visiting and communing with Land Spirits in the area. The message growing out of that work is simple enough. The ancestors 'in the land' are an essential component of what we call 'creativity' and if we lose touch with them completely we are cut off from any communion with our spiritual aspects – effectively dead in the sense of Jesus' comment, 'let the dead bury their dead'… The answer to this problem is simple enough. In the state of prayer we share qualities with the ancestors, so we need to pray together often. As I am a Baha'i I was told to use Baha'i prayer – you might be a Christian or a pagan, so do what comes naturally to you. It's the doing that matters – all else will flow from that.

Well, that is what has gone on since the articles ended. (Obviously I have left out much…) I hope all this will give you ideas to pursue on your own.

All reality is out there (or in there?) But we have to take the first step.

*Alan Royce 27.3.17*

## Bibliography *

**Borderlands:**
*European Paganism*, Ken Dowden
*The Tribe of Witches*, Stephen J. Yeates
*A Dreaming for the Witches*, Stephen J. Yeates
*Warriors of the Wasteland*, John Grigsby
Branwen Ferch Llyr – The Mabinogion – see the 'Cauldron Couple' section
Kecks, Keddles & Kesh, Michael Bayley for 'Briva' and other joys.

**St Joseph's Well and the Passage to the Tor:**
*The Architectural History of Glastonbury Abbey*, R. Willis
*An Architectural History of Glastonbury Abbey*, F. B Bond
*The Kennawell Biography of Frederick Bligh Bond, the Quest in Glastonbury*
Several old Glastonbury Guidebooks from the Avalon Library

**The Salmon's Leap:**
*The Apple Branch, A Path to Celtic Ritual, Alexei Kondratiev, 1988, Collins Press*
*Mysteries of the Dark Moon, Demetra George, 1992, Harper San Francisco*
*The Age of Arthur (Vol 1), John Morris, 1977, Phillimore & Co Ltd*
*The Mysteries of Mithras, Payan Nabarz, article in White Dragon No 20 1988*
*The Stone Salmon in Glastonbury Abbey who brought out the whole thing!*

**The Watching of the Rose:**
*The New Jerusalem*, Adrian Gilbert (British Israel and its roots)
*The Avalonians*, Patrick Bentham (a Glaston overview)
*Dion Fortune & The Inner Light*, Gareth Knight (Dion Fortune, Bligh Bond, &c.)
*The Misraim Service*, Rudolph Steiner (Steiner's Misraim connection)

*Modern Ritual Magic*, F. King (Felkin's links to Steiner)
*Iona*, Fiona Macleod, and *St Mary Magdalene*, Tau Malachi (the female Messiah)
*Glastonbury Scripts* and *Mystery of Glaston*, Frederick Bligh Bond (The Rose Stone)


**Roots of the Rune Tree:**
*The Lost Zodiac of The Druids*, Gregory A Clouter
*The Mysteries of Mithras*, Payam Nabarz
*Rudiments of Runelore,* Stephen Pollington
*The Circle of Stars*, Valerie J Roebuck
Extensive Google searches on 'Persian Calendar History'


**The Mystery of Mithras:**
*Manfred Clauss: The Roman Cult of Mithras*, Edinburgh University Press 2000, ISBN 0-7486-1396-X (a good scholarly overview).
*David Ulansey: The Origin of The Mithraic Mysteries – Cosmology & Salvation in The Ancient World*, Oxford University Press 1989, ISBN 0-19-506788-6 (an attempt to explain the origin and purpose of the cult).
*Roger Beck: The Religion of The Mithras Cult in The Roman Empire – Mysteries of The Unconquered Sun*, Oxford University Press 2006, ISBN 0-19-814089-4 (a deeper attempt to understand the cult's purposes and methods).
*Ian Ridpath: Star Tales*, Lutterworth Press 1988, ISBN 0-7188-2695-7 (useful contemporary star-lore).
*D. Jason Cooper: Mithras – Mysteries & Initiation Rediscovered,* Weiser 1996, ISBN 0-87728-865-8 (an occultist's attempt to understand the cult by comparison with similar modern occult groups).
*Payam Nabarz: Mysteries of Mithras, The Pagan Beliefs That Shaped The Western World*, Inner Traditions 2005, ISBN 1-59477-0271 (a useful modern attempt to revive the mystery).
*www.tertullian.org/rpearse/mithras/index.htm* (a collection of contemporary references to Mithraism).
*groups.yahoo.com/group/mithras*                                        -
*groups.yahoo.com/group/mithraeum* (discussion groups on academic study of Mithraism, and the practice of Mithraism as a renewed religion, respectively).

**The Serpent in the Bowl:**
For a different, and very useful, look at the Gundestrup Cauldron:
'The Lost Zodiac of the Druids', Gregory Clouter, 2003, Vega
Publications, ISBN 1-84333-635-9

For a more extensive look at the 'parts of the soul': the website of
John Opsopaus at http:\\www.cs.utk.edu/~Mclennan/BA/JO-
TEP.html

For Lucan references: Commenta Bernensis on Lucan 1.445

*the bibliographies are as they appeared in the original articles.*

*Acknowledgments*

My thanks go to Patrick Bentham, for his paradigm-changing book "The Avalonians"; to the people at Chalice Well, whose fascinating archives inspired the first of these writings; to Kat e Gooch, without whose dedication they would never have seen the light of day; to the folk at the Library of Avalon, who rescued them from the Flood; to my dear wife Pauline for at least half of the ideas roaming in this wilderness of words; to myriad others (Human and Otherworld) whose thoughts and proofs of guidance crop up everywhere therein(those I haven't mentioned in the various bibliographies, that is!).

*Alan Royce*

Printed in Great Britain
by Amazon